Getting Along

Skills for life-long love

Dear Liv,
with so much love,
Christopher ♡ Alyssa ☺
Anne

Christopher & Anne Ellinger

with Alyssa Lynes

BP

Belmarlin Press

Printed in the United States

ISBN-13: 978-1692051907
ISBN-10: 1692051903

Cover illustration and design by Dana Martin
Interior illustrations by Donna Cohen and Puneet Syal
Flow charts by Alyssa Lynes

Table of Contents

Acknowledgments

We are grateful for the substantial help from many friends: Dina Friedman for major editing, Ann Davis for assisting in re-writing the introduction, Pinal Maniar and Puneet Syal for late-night layout sessions of the manuscript, Dana Martin for the beautiful cover illustration and design, and Tonia Pinheiro for proofing. We also appreciate the enthusiasm and thoughtful comments of many other friends, including Amber Espar, Audrey Beth Stein, Betsy & Gail Leondar-Wright, Jonathan Stein, Michele Robbins, Richard Pendleton, Rob Kanzer, and Will Parish.

We acknowledge the many teachers who taught us formative personal growth and communication models. These include: Marshall Rosenberg for Nonviolent Communication, Jeannie Newman for adult educational design, various trainers from Movement for a New Society and Haymarket People's Fund for group facilitation, the Harvard Negotiation Project and the Cambridgeport Problem Center for conflict mediation training, Cherie Brown and the National Coalition Building Institute for diversity training, Ellen Deacon and Pamela Haines for Re-evaluation Co-counseling, Sandra Boston for Parent Effectiveness Training, Tom Yeomans for Psychosynthesis counseling, and Stephen Josephs for Neuro-Linguistic Programming (NLP).

We also appreciate our teachers in improvisational music, drama, and dance forms, including Jonathan Fox and Jo Salas for Playback Theatre, Randy Newswanger, Cynthia Winton-Henry and Phil Porter for Interplay, Thomas Cobb and the men's group for SpiritSong, Rhiannon for improvisational song, Martin Keogh, Angie Hauser, and others for contact improvisation dance. We're inspired by Anne's parents, Jan and David Slepian, whose gusto for life and love fed us.

In this second edition of the book we're so delighted that Alyssa Lynes has added valuable insights and tools from her experience with love.

Introduction

Staying in love

Falling in love is one of life's most desired experiences, without which our time on earth can seem a long slog across a lonely desert. Staying in love, however, is usually less poetic. It's more work than wonder, particularly if you live and work together as we have. How do you keep the mystery of romance alive if there's precious little space between you for any mysteries at all?

In 1981, when we first discovered the pleasure of being together, we forged a commitment not only to stay together, but also to work together to make the world a better place. We were long on idealism and painfully short on experience.

Bigger than just the two of us

Somehow, we did it. During our run of three decades, we have not only stayed together happily but also contributed to the world as a couple. In the 1990s, we created a journal called *More than Money* to stimulate new conversations about money, values, and ethical choices. This evolved into Bolder Giving, a nonprofit that promotes inspiring stories of people from across the economic spectrum who give far beyond the norm.

For years, most of the work was an uphill battle, relatively unacknowledged and under-funded. But now we can truthfully say that these two projects are helping to change the national conversation around giving and unleashing untold millions in charitable dollars. Our book, *We Gave Away a Fortune*, won an American Book Award and, after the difficult start-up years, Bolder Giving received breakthrough recognition from the Bill and Melinda Gates Foundation enabling its impact to soar.

We have now passed these beloved projects to the leadership of a new generation of philanthropists. We've gone on to build other social entrepreneurial projects that make our hearts sing: True Story Theater, which fosters community-building and healing through improvised performances of important real-life stories, Playback North America, a network to strengthen this kind of theatre across the continent, and Arts Rising, which promotes participatory arts and social change.

Relying fully on each other

Never could we have accomplished any of this without each other's daily involvement and support. We assisted each other through the daily drudgery and the most challenging times: when colleagues in the philanthropic world seemed to think we were just too weird, when we received a shocking rejection from an organization we fostered, and when our first child died at birth. (Happily, our beloved son Micah was born healthy a year later.) Through it all, we managed to keep living, working and loving each other.

What's your secret?

Decades ago, when we had been together a mere ten years, some friends asked, "How do you get along so well? Would you tell us your secret?" We responded by putting together *Getting Along*, a sheaf of photocopied pages containing our best relationship tools. We shared that compilation with many friends through the years and were gratified to hear how useful many people found it.

Twenty years passed: time spent raising our son, developing the projects described above, honing the skills we described in the original guide and inventing many more. We decided it would be exciting to cull the lessons we learned since that first writing and put them more attractively into the world with the benefit of electronic publishing. *Getting Along* is now the book you hold, which includes revised and further-developed pieces from our original work plus reflections on the hot topics of sexuality, money, parenting, working together, and aging.

We hope the curious mix in this guide offers a unique and useful window into long-term relationships. It's unusual to find in one book: step-by-step instruction in strengthening your communication, guidance for making tricky decisions, practical advice about money, tips on sexual exploration, antidotes to boredom in long-term relationships… yet all this and more is the territory of a shared life.

Worth the risk

We felt shy when we started writing this, aware that we were exposing the idiosyncratic workings of our life together. After all, we didn't create these tools for others; we developed them for our own relationship's needs. But we believe in shared learning and in taking risks, and so the potential gain from sharing our experience seems well worth the slight embarrassment.

We believe that everyone deserves abundant love and skillful support, whether they are simply building a fulfilling partnership or aspiring to offer additional gifts to the world. Our hope is that the skills in this book help you, dear readers, to strengthen all your relationships and to further your creative dreams.

Warmly,
Anne & Christopher

P.S. We are eager to know which parts of this guide you find most useful. After you have read some of it, please take a moment to give us your feedback and to share your own favorite practices. Please email us at Christopher@TrueStoryTheater.org. We would be delighted to learn from you.

Chapter 1

Get ready

Chapter 1: Get ready

Common concerns

You may be skeptical that communication skills can help in your particular situation. What works for some people is not always the right thing for others. However, if you have doubts like some of these examples below, we're hoping you may be pleasantly surprised by how useful some of these tools here will be to you.

My partner doesn't like to "process"

Many people have had painful experiences with "processing" in relationships. They might equate processing with talking through conflicts endlessly and fruitlessly, with being criticized under the guise of "being honest," or with stuffing genuine feelings to fit some manipulative self-help model. If that's the case, please know our intention is for the exercises to support genuineness.

I don't like structure

Sometimes, people don't like "processing" because they prefer other modes than talking, and they assume processing means words, words, and more words. Please adapt the exercises here to fit your individual learning styles. You can draw pictures, write instead of speaking, go for walks, cuddle, or stretch while talking, dance or act out your answers instead of speaking. Be creative!

Many people reject structured communication as too stilted or constraining. We agree that structure for its own sake is pointless; if you are doing fine without structure you probably don't need it! But if your relationship has recurring conflicts, or you feel less than fully heard and appreciated by your partner, then try-ing these new ways of communicating may help. Even if you have no communication "problems," taking time to explore new tools and models—especially if both of you practice them—can bring fresh ease, delight, and depth to your relationship. As you get good at using them the structure falls away and new ways of relating be-come increasingly natural.

My partner and I are so different

Naturally, it's simpler to get along when you have a lot of common-alities. The two of us are nearly the same age, and both Americans from secular Jewish families. We are also compatible in dozens of ways we didn't realize when we got together: from the kinds of movies, music, and food we most enjoy, to our energy levels, sleep rhythms, and ways of processing information. In these ways, getting along has been easy. If your relationship is straddling major differ-ences, such as age, religion, class, race, culture or language, it may be more difficult to create mutually acceptable styles for working out conflict. Yet developing a robust communication toolkit may be even more vital for the long-term health of your relationship.

Our situation is seriously bad

Stressful circumstances (such as unemployment, chronic illness, raising a disabled child) make it much harder to get along. Many situations such as abuse or addiction call for more immediate and basic resources than communication skills. Nonetheless, even in difficult circumstances, better communication can help, especially after you've addressed your crisis.

Beliefs matter

The practices in this guide are based on beliefs about human inter-action quite different from the ones the two of us were raised with. Perhaps you, too, were raised with assumptions like these:

It is not okay to ask directly for what you want.
Most emotions are disturbing and bad.
To make someone change, criticize or punish them.
In conflicts there are winners and losers.
People are the way they are; you can't change them.

In contrast, the models we work with are based on these beliefs:

Ask for what you want: *Discerning what you want and directly requesting it is essential for deep and genuine relationships.*

Emotions are natural: *Learning to skillfully express feelings can help us heal, experience being vibrantly alive, and communicate more fully.*

Encourage growth: *To best change someone's behavior, includ-ing your own, use empathy, appreciation, and encouragement.*

Find win-win solutions: *In most situations, you can find creative ways to meet everyone's needs.*

People can change: *You can skillfully help each other heal from past hurts and grow into your best selves.*

Because the ways of thinking and acting in this guide are developed from these beliefs, to some they may seem quite strange. We en-courage you to try them on anyway, and see whether they improve your relationships and wellbeing.

Stages of skill-learning

Think of a skill you learned that at first felt awkward and frustrating but eventually became easy. Perhaps driving a car... using new software... learning to cook... playing tennis. To learn new communication skills is no different. It takes practice and persistence to get through the early stages.

When we first we tried on new ways to communicate based on the new beliefs above, we often felt stupid and frustrated. So we developed the skill-learning model below to keep up our spirits as we moved through each stage. We hope the model helps you, too. Even in the early stages, we believe the rewards of these new practices can outweigh the discomforts.

Stages of constructive skill-learning

Stage 1: Accept confusion: In this first stage, you're often frustrated, not sure you even understand the basics. Remember this is totally natural. Expect it and don't be thrown.

Stage 2: Celebrate awkwardness: In the next stage, you know what you're trying to do but it often seems terribly belabored. Instead of quitting, you can congratulate yourself for reaching the awkward stage.

Stage 3: Relax into deliberateness: Now you can do the new skill, but only with concentration. Sometimes you remember the new behavior and sometimes you slip into the old. Again, there's no need to berate yourself when you lose it. Just know it's a normal part of the "deliberate" phase.

Stage 4: Notice the new normal: Suddenly, you're using the skill without even noticing. It just seems natural! Notice how you've changed, so you can appreciate the work you've put into it.

 We recommend you to start by practicing the new skills in this guide in relaxed situations. Even skills that appear simple can be tricky when you're upset—which, ironically, is when you need them the most. If it's touchy to practice with your partner, then recruit a friend to try them with you. Give yourself easy successes to start. Then work up to trying them in more tense times.

At first you might chafe against sounding "fake." Don't worry: the more you practice, the more flowing and natural these new ways of communicating will become.

Ready? Let's jump in!

Get ready: key points

Common concerns

> My partner doesn't like to process
> I don't like structure
> My partner and I are so different
> Our situation is seriously bad

Constructive beliefs

> Ask for what you want
> Emotions are natural
> Encourage growth
> Find win-win solutions
> People can change

Stages of skill learning

> Accept confusion
> Celebrate awkwardness
> Relax into deliberateness
> Notice the new normal

Chapter 2
Step out of upsets

Chapter 2: Step out of upsets

Basic commitments

To get along in any relationship, you need constructive ways to respond when you are *not* getting along. You'll be hugely helped by building a toolkit your partner shares: mutually agreed-upon language, concepts and processes that enable you to constructively resolve your differences without spiraling into big scenes or simmering into unexpressed resentments.

The skills in this section were mind-blowing to us when we first practiced them. Anne grew up in a "nice" family where open conflict was avoided at all costs; Christopher's was similar, except that at random times his father would explode in anger. Neither of us really knew how to work things out. Luckily, we both were excited to learn the personal growth and relationship communication concepts and skills below, so different from our upbringing.

If your partner is resistant to trying these new ideas, don't worry. They can revolutionize your relationship even if only you take them on. As the saying goes, it takes two to tango. Listen open-mindedly to what's behind your partner's reluctance. Give it time. Find friends who are interested and practice with them. Another great way to practice is to use the conflicts and upsets you have with yourself! Integrating even one of the practices into your relationship can bring greater ease and connection.

Say yes to conflict, no to drama

In order to use the tools in the section, you have to be willing to step out of your upsets. This doesn't mean sweeping issues under the rug or denying your feelings; it means letting go of high drama, unnecessary storm and thunder.

If you are someone who is attached to passionate fights for their energy and emotion, if fighting is how you feel alive and cared for, you might be afraid that letting go of your upset means your needs won't get heard.

But fights and conflict are not the same. While you may feel that fights are the most direct way to honestly communicate when you're in emotional pain, they are often not the most productive way to resolve conflict. Far too often, fights leave scars that are sadly unnecessary.

If you're accustomed to feeling close through fighting and making up, resolving conflicts peaceably may feel foreign and even dull at first. But relationships without dramatic upsets can still be full of great vitality and intimacy. Addressing conflict in your relationship offers a potential treasure chest of growth for you and your partner.

Letting go of upsets enables you to embrace conflict more readily when it arises. Instead of just fighting, you can actually hear each other, even when expressing deeply painful feelings. And through skillful listening, you can help each other meet the unmet needs that are causing the upset.

Choose a good time

It takes physical and emotional energy not to get swept into the other person's upset. It takes energy to listen accurately, to step out of yourself and empathize, and to be creative about solutions. Good timing makes an enormous difference. Often, attempts to resolve conflict go badly because neither partner has sufficient resources of spirit and energy at that time. If you and your partner are tangled in upset feelings and together you don't feel resourceful enough to deal with them well, then STOP. It might feel hard to resist fighting, but STOP until you can get the resources you need.

If you ask to postpone an important discussion until a better time, reassure your partner you are committed to processing together soon:

> *You know, I see you're really upset about this, and I do want to talk it over with you, but right now my head aches and I'm so tired that all I can think about is getting to bed. Can we talk about it in the morning? I could talk after dinner tomorrow, too, if we need more time.*

Or perhaps instead of postponing, you can ask for something that will give you the emotional slack you need:

> *Before we launch further into this, could we spend five minutes re-membering some of the fights we used to get into but have success-fully worked through? I need to feel more hopeful before taking on this challenge.*

> *Could we have this discussion while we walk outside? I think see-ing the beautiful fall leaves will help me listen better.*

> *I bet if I first took a 15 minute run, I'd handle this upset a whole lot better.*

> *Could you wait for me to shower and change my clothes? I promise I'll make time to talk afterwards.*

I know this is an important issue for us to work through. But I feel raw and tired from all the difficult talks we've had lately. Would you have the slack to rub my feet for 5 minutes while we're just quiet and listening to some soothing music? I need to feel better connected with you and myself before we take on another hard issue.

In order to agree to postpone, your partner may need:

- Reassurance that you're committed to addressing the issue.
- Explanation of why taking a break or doing something else will help.
- A chance to vent feelings for a few minutes first. Ask your partner to vent using sounds instead of words, so you don't get caught into the content.
- Help thinking about constructive things to do with upset feelings while waiting for you (e.g. write about her feelings; do something to help her feel more resourceful, too).
- A track record of following through on what you say you'll do (if you ask to postpone).

Frame a positive context

Before digging into the work of cleaning up upsets or resolving disagreements, give voice to those words that will support you and your partner to be your best selves with each other. Then, instead of being afraid of conflict and trying to avoid it, or falling into an old habit of scarring fights, you both may actually learn to welcome it.

Before we launch into discussing our conflict, I ask that you take a deep breath and remember a few things: Remember that I love you, and that I'm committed to taking to heart what you need and finding solutions that serve us both. Remember that we have gotten through difficult things before, and that we have excellent resources to get through whatever is before us now. I trust that working on these issues will teach us to better meet each of our needs and strengthen our partnership.

Aaah! Hearing any words like these – even one sentence!—in the midst of a painful conflict can help both parties sigh with relief.

Take brief turns

Here's a common difficulty: you're trying to work out a disagreement, but instead you both keep upsetting each other. Each phrase one of you says ticks the other off, making it hard for the other person to listen. It's like you're both in a slippery dark barrel, and each time you try to crawl towards the light you slip back.

When you both are upset at the same time, the first step is for one of you to say, "Stop! Let's take turns." Then follow this process:

The person speaking is the one whose needs are on the table. The listener is the helper.

Set a timer. Each turn needs to be short enough that the listener can stay in the listening role and not get drawn into the content. Start with 30 seconds each. Then one minute each. Then go to two minutes each. Then five minutes each. By then, perhaps one of you will feel calm enough to do some real listening.

The person more upset talks first. Then switch. You can go back and forth as many times as needed.

The speaker's job:

If you have a lot of pent up emotions, you might take the first turn or two to release them. Use sounds instead of words. Sounds are more expressive and far easier for other person to listen to without getting reactive. "Grrrr! GRRRRR!!!"

Speak about yourself, not your partner. Name your own feelings and needs. "I feel irritated! I need rest." Not: "You're mean. You're noisy and inconsiderate!"

Beware of starting a sentence with "I feel you..." That's likely to be a projection onto the other person or a judgment of him, not a feeling. Describe your partner's behavior without labeling him. Give specific observations not interpretations. "When you left dishes in the sink last night," instead of: "when you don't want to be bothered washing up."

The listener's job:

If you're just learning this skill or feel really triggered, don't say a word while listening. If you've practiced a lot and are reasonably calm, you can encourage the speaker with empathetic sounds or phrases.

Keep breathing. Try to keep your face as relaxed and accepting as possible. Remember: this is a hurting person whom you love.

Let your partner's sharp emotions "roll off your shoulders," not cut into your mind and body. Remember that even if they are blaming you, the speaker is responsible for their own upset, just as you are the one responsible for yours.

Notice what gets you triggered. Name your feelings to yourself as they bubble up, but don't blurt them out.

Stay attentive to the other hurting person. If you get too caught up in your own feelings and needs, ask to switch roles.

Be patient. It may take a few rounds of this for you to discern the real needs beneath the upset. Even if it feels emotionally strenuous, keep the faith that this process is quicker and more effective than emotional fights, or leaping to "solutions" by pretending irrational feelings aren't there.

At all times, you need to know whose needs are on the table. It can't be both of you simultaneously. Don't get into problem solving together until you've done enough short back-and-forth that you can really listen. If you start interrupting each other, go back to timed turns. Once both of you are calm and feel fully heard, you might try the problem solving method described next, to come up with creative ways to meet both of your needs.

Win-win problem solving

In our haste to "fix" a problem, it's easy leap to solutions before we may actually understand the nature of the problem. Then we're resentful that our well-intentioned help was shot down and we're discouraged from offering further ideas.

The first skill in creative problem solving is being willing to not know the answer, but instead to patiently listen as different pieces of the problem become clear. Only when each person's needs are thoroughly understood can you design a solution that creatively satisfies everyone's needs. You have to let yourself trust that such a "win-win" resolution is possible, and not give in to the urge to settle quickly by compromise. Compromises often lead to lingering resentments, because in compromising you give up some of what you want or need. When a win-win solution has been implemented, all the important needs are satisfied and there is nothing left to resent. The "problem" has been transformed into an opportunity to better understand both yourself and your partner.

Here's how the process works:

Win-win problem solving:

Step 1: Listen to both of your needs.
Step 2: Brainstorm creative ways to meet the needs.
Step 3: Synthesize a proposal and work out concerns.
Step 4: Try your solutions for a while; then evaluate.

For example, many arguments start like this: each person expresses feelings indirectly, labels each other, and leads with solutions that seem to be direct opposites.

> *Diane: Christine, why do you always want to read just as we go to bed? You only think of yourself. You know your reading keeps me up! Besides, you'll be grumpy in the morning from lack of sleep. Come on, turn out the light and snuggle with me.*

> *Christine: Nagging me doesn't make me want to snuggle. I so enjoy reading in bed before sleep. Just close your eyes, ignore the light, and you'll be asleep in no time.*

Listen to both of your needs

The first step of constructive problem solving is to talk about each of your specific needs, leaving solutions aside for the moment. Here is an abbreviated example:

> *Diane: Please tell me what's important to you about reading in bed.*

> *Christine: Well, it's about the only time all day that feels like it's just for me. After reading for fifteen minutes I can go right to sleep,*

but if I try to sleep without it, my mind goes round and round about unfinished work and hassles of my day. I like reading in bed more than other places because it's cozy and warm, and it has the best light—and also, because I get to be close to you!

Diane first tells Christine what she understood of Christine's experience. Then she asks Christine to listen to her feelings.

Diane: I feel hurt when you crawl into bed and grab a book. I imagine you're avoiding me. I want to snuggle and talk about our day. It's hard for me to sleep while you read, and not just because of the light, either. Every time you turn the page, it wakes me up. You say you need only fifteen minutes, but sometimes you read for over an hour, and then I have to deal with your grumpiness the next morning.

Brainstorm options

Once you understand all the component needs, brainstorm together lots of possible solutions that might meet the needs. For now, refrain from reacting (even with your facial expression) to any of the ideas. Just generate lots of them. Be silly and make each other laugh. Crazy ideas help loosen your minds to new possibilities.

Diane and Christine's idea list:
- D. wear earplugs.
- C. read in living room.
- D. come to bed after C. has read 15 minutes
- C. snuggle and talk with D. for 10 minutes before reading
- D. do the dishes more often so C. can read after dinner.
- Buy a warm quilt to make for cozy reading in living room
- C. set a watch beeper and stop reading after 15 minutes
- Instead of reading, C. listen to story tapes using earphones.
- C. read short stories instead of novels; stop at end of one story.
- D. knit and listen to music with earphones while C. reads
- C. plans how to be cheerful the next day, if reads over 30 min.

Synthesize a proposal

After generating lots of possibilities, both partners can discuss which suggestions might work for them, and together work up a proposal. There's no need to talk about solutions that either party rejects. If there aren't enough attractive options, brainstorm some more.

> *Diane: I'd be willing to try knitting and listening to music while you read. Or coming to bed after you've read a while.*

> *Christine: I'd actually like help to stop reading after fifteen minutes. I never set a timer because I didn't want to wake you! I'd love to snuggle and talk after reading, as long as we went to sleep within ten or fifteen minutes.*

Evaluate

At a determined point in the future, discuss how the solutions are working. If the solutions aren't satisfying all the needs (as many will not because the real needs may require more exploration), simply go back into problem-solving mode, taking the new information into account.

> *Diane: I feel hopeful about this plan. Let's try it this week and talk again on the weekend to see if we want to change anything.*

Pattern interruption

Sometimes we get "triggered" by certain ways our partner holds or expresses himself—a certain tone of voice, a tense holding of the jaw. Anything that will interrupt those automatic triggers will help break the tension. Together, try out different ways to jiggle the energy between you and notice which actions work the best. Below are some suggestions to get you started.

Play with body habits

Sometimes when dealing with a minor conflict, simply making a change in your body or voice can help you both lighten up. See what it's like to continue the discussion while:

- *Talking back to back or leaning against each other*
- *Standing on chairs*
- *Making your voices extra high or low pitch*
- *Talking in accents*
- *Making strange faces*
- *Talk with your faces scrunched up*

Laughter is great!

Reverse roles

Sometimes you and your partner may feel locked into opposite positions on an issue. You may be dismayed to find that talking about it doesn't lessen the differences; in fact, the more you talk about the issue, the more polarized you become, until the discussion starts to feel very repetitive. "Ucch! When I say this, you always say that."

A powerful way to reverse this polarization is to literally reverse the positions that you've each taken. For a mutually agreed-upon period of time, you and your partner each pretend that your position is now what the other person was previously advocating. For the role reversal to work, you have to play the new role as honestly as you can, without the least bit of mockery. Remember that this is just an exercise. You don't have to agree with the part you are playing for this period of time. Just be true to it.

Reversing roles can relieve tensions, deepen your understanding of each other's perspective, and loosen your positions by allowing you to voice unexpressed parts of yourselves. Playing opposite roles can turn a struggle against each other into a fun way to reach together for mutual understanding.

There are many ways to play with role reversals. You can try switching roles just for just a few minutes, or you can decide that for several days you will express each other's positions on an issue instead of your own. You can choose to make your role reversals as genuine and accurate as you can, or you can play with them through light-hearted exaggeration. For example, if you rarely initiate love-making, in a genuine role reversal you might now say, "Let's make love tonight, okay? I miss being close to you," and your partner, the one who always initiates, now acts reluctant. "Oh dear, I really have work to do..." Or to help shift tensions, you could agree to add playfulness and drama to the role reversal. "Darling! I must have you! Now! Yes here, on the kitchen table..." "I think I'd like a few months of celibacy, OK?"

Play with it! After the reversals, talk about how they felt and any insights you gained.

We used role reversals during a touchy period when Anne wanted to get pregnant but Christopher wanted to wait. The situation was tense. We switched roles for a few days, playing it up big. Christopher would say, "Beloved, when you get home, I'll have picked out possible names for our baby!" Anne would demur. "Honestly, I don't think I'm ready!" After a few days of playing with this role reversal, we were able to have a much more productive discussion about the decision, each feeling looser about our positions.

Own responsibility

At the start of an argument, take responsibility for whatever truth is in your partner's accusations, as soon as you can. This can be a dramatic way to interrupt your pattern. "It's true, I was the one emptying the dish drain when your favorite mug fell. I want to do something about it. Can I replace it or reimburse you?" Just step over your defensiveness and do it. After you have taken responsibility, your partner will be more open to discussing extenuating circumstances. "You know, I've been asking the family for weeks not to pile more dishes in the drainer once it's full. And when your mug fell, the baby was crying and I was carrying her. She was the one to knock it out of the drainer."

It may feel like swallowing pride, but this simple act will eliminate many hours of unnecessary fighting. "Yes, I was late." "It's true, I did raise my voice." "You're right, I wasn't thinking about you when I made that appointment." Take responsibility first, and then discuss the rest of the situation.

Forgive

Another powerful way to interrupt a pattern of upset or resentment is by asking for or offering forgiveness. "I'm sorry if I hurt your feelings by my grumpiness today. Will you forgive me?" or "I forgive you for hurting my feelings this morning." Initially, your partner may feel uncomfortable: "Don't apologize, I don't think you did anything wrong," or "Don't blame me, I didn't do anything wrong." You can explain that the point is not blame, but to help you both feel that your hurts and needs count.

Paradoxically, asking for forgiveness can be healing in situations where you feel judgmental toward your partner. "I get terribly resentful when you leave your dishes unwashed in the sink, and I really hate harboring those feelings toward someone I adore. Will you forgive me for thinking negatively about you?" Expressing forgiveness can open you both to exploring the deeper issue. If you express forgiveness first before asking, "Can we talk again about kitchen cleanup and each of our needs? I'll make an effort to put aside my judgmental attitudes," your discussion will likely go more easily.

Forgiveness is potent when practiced regularly. You don't need to wait for a special occasion! Assuaging the little hurts means they don't need to build up to huge issues. Plus it helps to get in the forgiveness habit, so it's less hard to offer in a charged situation.

Playfully claim the blame

This is especially useful when your partner is in a stew of upset that has nothing to do with you (e.g. bad traffic, a nasty interaction at work, losing her car keys). You playfully claim ALL the blame.

> *Beloved, it's all my fault! I should have protected you better! Please forgive me!*

Often this releases gales of relieving laughter. Your partner's role is to respond,

> *Yeah, you jerk! It's all your fault! Why didn't you know I needed to go to the dentist (even though I didn't tell you I had a toothache) before we left on this vacation?!"*

Why does this work? Often, when we're upset about something we long for someone to blame (even though we know that's not constructive). Often, we blame ourselves but wish we didn't. Or we have the urge to blame our partner, even if the fault was 99% our own. When partners assume more than their share of the responsibility, they are indirectly empathizing with this desire to blame and cutting through any self-blame we have layered on to the already-painful situation.

Note: your partner needs to have read the exercise so they understand what you're doing. Also, you have to sound sincere, not sarcastic. The technique comes from a peer counseling method called "Re-evaluation Co-counseling" that teaches many forms of emotional release. See the Resources section for this and other training in skillful empathy. We also recommend Nonviolent Communication developed by Marshall Rosenberg and Leader (or Parent) Effectiveness Training developed by Thomas Gordon.

Love the uglies

When we feel angry... depressed... grumpy... upset... most of us not only have to deal with these uncomfortable feelings, but we're also mad at ourselves for feeling and acting that way. We feel ugly and unlovable, which only makes us sink deeper into our bad mood. If, on top of all that, someone we care about criticizes us for our feelings (when we're probably already trying as hard as we can to feel better) it's the opposite of what we need. We desperately need a helpful hand, not a kick.

One way to get out of this downward cycle is to practice "loving the uglies" so the uglies don't scare us. Set aside five minutes to practice with a partner when one of you is in a good mood and the other is down (but not down about you).

> *When Al makes an ugly growl, Betsy beams at him with total love and approval. Next Al storms and stomps and Betsy smiles with delight saying "Aw, there must be something you need!" Al snarls, "I hate comments like that!" Betsy beams acceptance, with a gentle "Feeling bad, huh. Must be miserable."*

Sometimes you can even talk directly to the uglies. "Hey, you bad mood, let my friend go and stop torturing her." You can develop pet names for each other's favorite uglies, such as "Mr. Anxiety," or "Madam Perfection."

Loving the uglies can help both parties lighten up. Be prepared for laughter and tears: because most of us received disapproval when we felt bad when we were growing up, getting approval now goes deep into the heart.

The Glitch Process

This is one of the most elegant processes we've come up with. It has saved us from long ugly conflicts many times! However, it is an advanced skill, requiring proficiency both with win-win problem solving described above, and with skillful empathy, described in the next chapter. With practice, "The Glitch Process" may become as quick as the times below, but give it more ample time when you are first learning it.

> *George and Francis have been invited to a 6:30pm dinner party. On the car ride there they get upset with each other. They pull up to the house at 6:30 sharp, both fuming.*

What can they do besides go in and feel hostile all night, or start arguing in the car, where they'll probably end up hopelessly late and still upset? They can use the the Glitch Process! Here's how it works:

Step 1: Agree

They agree to do the Glitch Process. 10 seconds.

> *George: I know we're late for the party but could we please use our glitch process before we go in to feel better connected?*
> *Francis: OK, let's do it! I'm going first!*

Step 2: Vent

They take turns to each vent strong feelings without using words. Each partner listens without responding. 1 minute each.

> *Francis, weeping: Grrrrr!! (etc.)*
> *George: pounds the steering wheel (etc.)*

Step 3: Empathize

They make their best guess as to what the other person is feeling and do their best to express it empathetically and genuinely. The other person gives information to help the empathy be more accurate. 3 minutes each.

> *George: Francis, I know you have an intense headache. I bet you wish we didn't have to visit with these folks, is that right? And you could really use some time to yourself? (Francis can add or correct his empathetic guesses.)*

> *Francis: I imagine you're bummed because you wanted to get there early to surprise your friends and are frustrated that I wasn't ready when I said I would be? Is that right? (George can add or correct her empathetic guesses.)*

Step 4: Problem-solve

Based on the needs they heard through empathizing, they come up with creative solutions together about the issue. 2-5 minutes.

> *George: How about I go in now but you rest in the car for a while to ease your headache. Would that help?*

> *Francis: I think it would. Then I'll try to enjoy the party for an hour, but if I'm still miserable after that, could we leave without a fuss?*

> *George: I can agree to that. I'll make a date to connect with my friends hosting the party another time soon.*

Step 5: Appreciate

They express appreciations for each other. 1 minute.

> *Francis, thank you being willing to come, even these aren't your friends. It means a lot to me that we're willing to reach out to them even when you're feeling so bad.*
>
> *George, I appreciate your asking to take this time to process; I feel better. Thanks for being willing to leave early.*

The issue may not feel perfectly resolved, but chances are they both feel a whole lot better. It's probably only about 6:45 (given slack time on each step), just fashionably late, and they're likely to actually enjoy the party.

Step out of upsets: key points

Basic commitments

Say yes to conflict, no to drama
Choose a good time
Frame a positive context
Take quick turns

Win-win problem-solving

1 Listen to both of your needs
2 Brainstorm options
3 Synthesize a proposal
4 Evaluate

- from Thomas Gordon, Parent Effectiveness Training

Interrupting patterns of upset

Play with body habits
Reverse roles
Own responsibility
Forgive
Playfully claim the blame
Love the uglies

The Glitch Process

1: Agree to do the Glitch Process.
2: Vent feelings without words.
3: Empathize with the other person's feelings.
4: Problem-solve together about the issue.
5: Appreciate each other and the process.

Chapter 3
Grow through compassion

Chapter 3: Grow through compassion

Many relationships sour because people want their partners to be different in some way, and they don't know how to support that to happen. They either criticize and nag at each other, or instead try to keep their negative thoughts to themselves. In either case, the result is not likely to be growth and harmony, but instead conflict or chilly distance.

This hefty chapter walks you through the skills of giving and receiving appreciation and empathy: two essential building blocks of loving, healthy, growing relationships. Once you and your partner gain proficiency in these delicious exchanges, you can apply those skills to respectfully help each other change, which is the focus of the final section of this chapter.

Appreciation

We believe that most people are under-appreciated most of the time. The norm in society is to criticize and complain, rather than praise. In our culture, we rarely give explicit appreciation, and we're certainly not supposed to *ask* for appreciation. That's "fishing for compliments" and considered in very bad taste.

However, while this may be the norm in society at large, it doesn't have to be the norm in your relationship. Learning to exchange plentiful, genuine appreciation can give great pleasure as well as add to your bonding.

You or your partner may feel resistant at first to a structured appreciation process. You might feel that you don't deserve the appreciation... that it doesn't count if it's not spontaneous... that it's hard to let go of resentments... that the whole thing is embarrassing. To ease these feelings, at the start of each practice take a few minutes each to express whatever resistance you feel to giving or receiving appreciation, making sure to simply listen without response when the other partner is speaking. Then leap over these resistances and appreciate each other. Laughter or tears are fine.

Practice abundantly

Set aside a specific time for you and your partner to practice appreciations. Even once a week for ten minutes can start to build the skill and habit. Once you feel warmed up to exchanging appreciations, integrate them abundantly into your daily life. Here are some of the many ways you can use appreciation to sweeten your life together:

Notice everyday gifts

Every day, no matter how "basic" it is for one of you to take on a certain responsibility, take time to acknowledge each other's effort on your collective behalf. Regular appreciation and gratitude makes living together a treat.

> *"Thanks for doing the dishes, Crystal."*
> *"Thanks for cooking, James."*
> *"Thanks for making the bed, Pedro."*
> *"Thanks for changing that diaper, Yolanda."*

You may think, "This is silly, I shouldn't need thanks for what I do all the time." But even if you don't feel as if you *need* appreciation, you might be surprised at how good it feels to receive it. Accept the appreciation simply, by saying "You're welcome" or "Thanks for thanking me." No deflection (such as "I didn't do such a good job" or "It's no big deal") is allowed. The whole exchange takes about five seconds.

Relieve tensions

Exchanging appreciations can be a powerful way to reduce resentments and to ease tension. You can use appreciations both as a ritual at the end of the day as well as when you notice distance between you. Practice directly offering it: "Is there anything you'd like appreciation for?" Practice directly asking to receive it: "Would you be willing to give me appreciation? Especially for..."

In any relationship, there are times when partners do unequal work. To reduce possible resentments, the partner doing less can acknowledge and appreciate the other person's contribution, framing the extra work as a gift to the relationship rather than a solitary burden.

> *Thanks for getting up in the night to nurse the baby, Sultana. I sure appreciate it.*

Appreciation is particularly soothing after working out a conflict, or in the middle of a difficult conversation when you both need a boost to keep going.

> *I'm feeling pretty raw from discussing this issue. Could we exchange appreciations for a few minutes before continuing?*

Relish similarities and differences

Some people choose partnerships based on the comfort of similarities; others choose partnerships based on the stimulation of differences. Yet similarities can feel dull as well as sweet; differences can be grating as well as enlivening. Using the "even though" format below we can acknowledge the challenge while giving the balm of specific appreciation.

> *Pauline, even though we cook together almost every day, I never take for granted how satisfying it is to enjoy our food. (Appreciating a similarity)*

> *George, even though I like the freedom to be a little messy, I do appreciate how much you help us keep a tidy, serene, and beautiful home. (Appreciating a difference)*

When appreciating differences, take care to offer appreciation without mixing in unmet needs or criticism.

Reinforce the positive

A daily practice of exchanging appreciations can help you and your partner focus on and strengthen what is right in your lives, instead of letting you be preoccupied with what is wrong, missing, or undone.

> *Michaela, what are 3 things you appreciate about:*
> *- how your life is on track?*
> *- our relationship?*
> *- what a good mother you are?*
> *- being alive in these interesting times?*

Support personal growth

Many of us not only repeat to ourselves what is wrong with the world, but what is wrong with *ourselves*. We have rehearsed negative messages about ourselves for so long that we rarely even notice that we're doing it. It doesn't work to simply try and shut off the negativity recording. We need to replace them with new messages, ones that are vigorously practiced until they seem more real than the old self-put-downs. You can invite your partner to voice self-appreciation for ways they're trying to grow:

> *Anne, what are three things you appreciate about how well you take care of your stuff? (Asked by Christopher because he knows she's trying to be less absent-minded.)*
>
> *Christopher, what are three things you appreciate about how calm and relaxed you were this week? (Asked by Anne because she knows he's working to be less anxious.)*

If it is hard to see your own progress, it can sometimes help to put your self-appreciation in an "even though" format:

> *Even though I lost my temper with the kids yesterday, I do appreciate that there were three times this week I felt like yelling at them but didn't. I'm moving in the right direction.*

Savor being together

Cultivating a habit of daily appreciations can dispel taking each other's presence for granted. Appreciations help us wake up to how wondrous a gift our moments together actually are. Many couples do this in their first few months together, when they're still awed by the newness of being with each other. We encourage you to deliberately develop this as an ongoing practice, no matter how many years and decades you have been together.

Imagine how special you feel when, after coming home from a stressful day at work, your partner leaps up from his desk to hug you and says, "I'm so happy to see you! I love being with you!"

Increase your appreciation skill

Have you ever had the experience of someone giving you an appreciation, but instead of feeling closer to the person you feel embarrassed or alienated? Or perhaps you've been the giver, and had the feeling that an appreciation you gave seemed to bounce off the recipient's surface, having no impact. How disappointing! Yet at other times, an appreciation can make your whole day, or touch your friend so deeply she weeps. What makes the difference?

There's an art to giving and receiving deeply nourishing appreciations. To make your appreciations more effective, work to embody qualities described below. Although these qualities are described from the giver's point of view, the recipient can also take the lead and request them. If you tend to be emotionally contained (because of sub-culture, family history, or personality) you may prefer to modify the tools in this section. Any appreciation is better than none! So don't let these more adventurous skills discourage you from giving simple appreciations in your own style.

Connect

If you want your appreciation to hit home, make sure it's a good time for both of you to let it in. Take the time needed to connect to your heart and to fully express what you're feeling.

Basic appreciation: Thanks for coming home early to help me, Jolie (said while Jolie is distracted putting away her coat).

Connective appreciation: (Taking Jolie's hands and making eye contact) Jolie, it means a lot to me that you left work early today to help me with my work crunch.

Disclose what's meaningful to you

Sometimes appreciations fall flat when they are vague, positive judgments about the other person: "You're so beautiful," or "What a smart decision," or "I admire your bravery!" Being judged, even if positively, often falls short of providing the full nourishment that skillful appreciation provides. Instead, try to name very specifically the behavior or quality you're appreciating so the listener clearly pictures what you're referring to. Then take the time to describe vulnerably why it's meaningful to you.

Basic appreciation: Jolie, you are a life saver! My hero!

Specific and self-disclosing appreciation: Jolie, I'm grateful you came home early to help me. I often feel alone with work. In my family growing up, any requests for help were seen as weakness. Your willingness to come help me feels healing as well as helpful.

Start with empathy

Beginning with empathy for your partner's feelings can help her let appreciation sink in, especially if she is stressed or distracted.

Basic appreciation: Wow, Jolie, I appreciate your coming home early to help me!

Empathetic appreciation: Wow, Jolie, you left work early. I imagine that might have been hard, given how pressured you've been lately. You coming home early to help me is especially meaningful to me since I know how much work you yourself have. Thank you!

Invite dialogue

Communication requires a "feedback loop" to feel complete. When you give an appreciation and then invite response, the conversation goes deeper.

> *Request for feedback: Jolie, anything you want to say after hearing those appreciations?*

> *Response: Well, you're right that I'm stressed at work, but that made it easy to leave. I wanted to get out of there. I forgot it's hard for you to ask for help, since it's easy for me. I'm glad my coming home means so much to you! I really didn't realize it.*

Discover your partner's "love language"

We've focused here on the craft of giving and receiving verbal appreciations, but words are not the only, or necessarily the most important, way to express love. The book and website *The Five Love Languages* can help you to discern which modes of expression are most potent for you and your loved ones: words of affirmation, acts of service, receiving gifts, quality time, and physical touch. (And of course, there are far more ways to express love than these five.)

It can be eye opening to compare notes with your partner about which "love languages" hit home and which ones don't. Anne feels hugely loved when Christopher brings her a snack midday... and she doesn't care the least about gifts, not even on birthdays or anniversaries. Have you been expressing love through your words, when what your beloved needs to feel loved most may be a backrub? Once you've deciphered each other's preferred ways to feel loved, you can give each other what the other most craves.

Empathy

Understand what empathy is and isn't

We want our partners to understand our feelings. Being told: "you shouldn't feel that way," usually leaves us feeling angry and hurt, and holding onto our feelings even more. Empathy, on the other hand, helps us let go of difficult feelings and move on.

We are often reluctant to empathize with each other because we confuse empathy with agreement. Empathizing simply means letting someone know you understand how they feel. It *does not* mean you support what they feel. It doesn't mean you agree with the reasons behind their feelings. Empathy means you can put yourself in their shoes and imagine accurately what is going on inside them, whether or not you agree.

Regularly ask for and offer empathy

Like all the skills in this guide, empathy may feel awkward and artificial at first. (Notice that now we're empathizing with what you might be feeling in reading this.) It will become natural over time. Try it first when you're both calm. As you get more proficient, you can experiment applying the balm of empathy when you or the other person is upset.

Ask for empathy:

> *Before you give your own viewpoint, it would really help me to know you've understood my feelings. Would you reflect back to me what I just said, especially the feeling part?*

Offer empathy:

> *Would you like me to say what I understand, before I respond to what you just said?*

Be Authentic

Empathy expressively reveals what you imagine your partner is experiencing. It is *not* just saying, "I understand how you feel" in a dutiful monotone. It sounds like: "I bet you felt frustrated being in that traffic jam, and probably anxious that I might be angry at you for being late!" or "Seems like you felt mad and hurt when I left without saying goodbye!" Make sure that your voice and manner genuinely expresses the emotion you're describing.

Expect to try and try again

Sometimes when you try to empathize with your partner she may say (passionately) "No, that's not what I feel!" If you can respond without being defensive, you can keep the focus on your partner. Say simply, "What *do* you feel? I want to understand." Once she has expressed herself, try empathizing again to see if you've got it. "So you weren't angry; you were very frustrated. Not because I forgot the groceries, but because you were counting on baking something special for Louise's party." Perhaps this time she will say, "Yeah. Well. Sort of. You got the first part right, but you forgot to say..." Listen, and then try again. "Oh! You were frustrated because you wanted my *help* baking for Louise, and I came home too late to help you." "Yes, that's it!"

As with appreciation, any empathy is better than none, so don't hold back. But don't be too surprised if the first awkward attempts at empathy are inaccurate and so a little painful. To be empathized with fully and accurately feels as exquisite as getting a long cool drink when you're parched with thirst. Keep working at it until you and your partner feel complete.

Mirror intense feelings

When your partner feels something intensely it can miss the mark to simply use words to empathize. Taking care to be sincere, join in with great expressiveness—perhaps even what may seem like exaggeration—to show you really get the full intensity of how it feels to your partner.

> *Weak joining: Janice, you must feel a bit disappointed to lose your mother's picture.*
>
> *Strong joining: Oh Janice, I mourn with you! I know how much that photo meant to you!*

You can also ask for more intense empathy.

> *Weak request for joining: I got the promotion! You can congratulate me.*
>
> *Strong request for joining: I got the promotion! Let's jump up and down and scream for a few minutes to celebrate!!!*

Sometimes it's enough to respond to invitations with a friendly nod or a murmur. But other times, our habitual ways of responding just won't do. Consider the following scene:

> *Elaine: I'd love us to plan a time to exchange massage this weekend. It's been too long.*
>
> *Jamie: Sure, that'd be nice. I'm not free this weekend, though.*

Responding in an extra expressive and empathetic way sometimes can make a big difference to your partner, especially when they have particularly strong feelings about something. Since vibrant responsiveness is rarely a daily habit, it takes practice. Either party can ask for a redo.

> *Jamie: Hmm ... Elaine, I see you look a little upset. Would you like me to give you a more responsive answer? OR*

Elaine: Hey Jamie, I felt vulnerable making that massage request. Are you actually interested? Would you be willing to make it clear to me if you are?

Jamie: Sorry to give a distracted response! Yes, I'm interested, and yes, it has been a long time. I'm sorry I haven't had more attention for you. This weekend I'm flat out finishing that grant proposal, but I'd love to join you next Wednesday night. Does that work for you?

For some people upsets can be put into perspective by exaggerated empathy. It's important that your partner understands what you're doing so she doesn't feel made fun of.

You were stuck in bad traffic for an hour?? How harrowing!!

To us, the word "harrowing" describes extreme circumstances – like a brush with death. Using it playfully like this helps us gain perspective that bad traffic isn't actually a crisis while also empathizing with how much we hate it. We often ritually acknowledge each other's tensions with the phrase, "how harrowing!"

Helping each other change

Here is a classic touchy situation, especially in a long-term relationship: You love your mate, but you wish she would change in certain ways, perhaps minor, perhaps major. "Be more ambitious." "Stop slouching." "Be less self-critical." "Learn to close the kitchen door without banging it." "Be on time."

You try to push aside your critical feelings, but eventually your annoyance leaks out. You try to talk it out, but your mate is quite defensive (even if she agrees with you, in theory). She doesn't change her behavior, and soon it's a sore point between you, a source of all-too-familiar arguments, hurt feelings, chilly avoidance, and even relationship break-ups.

Our relationship almost ended in year five when we were mired in these patterns. Anne thought if she could only criticize Christopher effectively enough—if he just understood how much pain she was in and how badly she needed him to change—then of course he'd be motivated enough to change. Instead, he felt defensive and abandoned with his difficulties.

Luckily, we discovered that the key to helping your partner change is to keep clear about whose needs are being addressed. We dug ourselves out of our destructive criticism patterns by designing Positive Growth Campaigns, described below.

Positive Growth Campaigns

Step 1: Take time alone to each write two lists. First, what are some ways you want to change? Second, what are some ways you want your partner to change?

Step 2: Note where your lists overlap. See where a change you want for your partner is also a change they want for themselves. Select one area for each person to create a "positive growth campaign." See Step 4 for where your lists differ.

Step 3: The person aiming to change takes daily small steps and receives abundant appreciation for any moves in the desired direction, no matter how small. The person supporting the change acts as cheerleader and takes any frustrations elsewhere. See tips below.

Step 4: Notice where your two lists differ: where you wish your partner would change but they don't care to, or where they want a change in themselves that you don't support. Discuss these items to discover if, after listening to each other, they become goals you share in common (or need acceptance of how you are now).

Where your goals remain different, learn how to constructively handle your own reactions. It is valuable to let your partner know how and why her behavior affects you, and to get her thinking about how to meet your needs. But be clear this is a discussion about you, not about your partner.

Tips for the person doing the changing

Start small. To achieve a change in behavior or personality, even a small one, usually takes consistent, long-term effort.

Strengthen your resolve to change. One way is to write down five reasons your life is hurt by the lack of change, five reasons why your life would benefit from the change, and five reasons why you believe you can change (such as people who can help you, strengths you have, past successes you can build on.) Read these lists frequently, and add to them.

Break your goal into small steps. As you take these steps expect to fall short again and again, especially if you're reaching for a substantial change. Forgive yourself and recommit to making the change.

Bring friends into the campaign. The more friends know what you're trying to do, the better. Coach them in positive reinforcement techniques, below. Take time with good friends to express and release whatever frustration, hopelessness, or other feelings that get in your way of taking action, so you don't need to only lean on your partner.

Tips for the person supporting the other's change:

Appreciate every little step in the right direction. If possible, do this daily. Be a consistent, genuine cheerleader.

Help your partner appreciate her own successes, no matter how small. You can design question games that help her recognize the good ways she's changing. For instance, for someone learning to speak up for herself, you might ask, "What are three things you appreciate about how assertive you are?" or "What are three ways you spoke up for yourself this week?"

Take negative feelings elsewhere. Do not take them to your partner. If you have a backlog of frustrated feelings about your partner's lack of change—say, anger about how your own life is affected, fear that change will never happen, or wild impatience with her slow progress—express them in your journal, to a counselor, or to someone who doesn't personally know your partner. If you must vent to a friend who knows both of you, be sure to protect the relationships. "Could I have three minutes to complain about Ki? You know I love her and nothing I'm about to say is serious. I just need to release some frustration. Is that OK? Please hold what I'm saying in confidence."

Stick with it. Expect that the change will be longer and slower than you might wish. Forgive your partner's failures, help her recommit, and help her do problem solving that puts her in the driver seat. Remember, people are often unsuccessful in trying to change because they get frustrated and give up, especially if they're criticized by their loved ones instead of encouraged. Most people need massive doses of support and positive reinforcement to change. You can provide that.

Example when both partners want the same change

Raiz' unconscious habit of chewing his lower lip drives Sophia crazy. She's especially embarrassed by it when they're in public. When they compared lists of things they wanted to change, she was pleased that this was something he wanted to change, too. He especially wanted to change the underlying cause of this habit: the chronic anxiety he carried in his body.

Together, Sophia and Raiz designed a positive personal growth campaign to address his anxiety and its symptoms such as lip chewing. He took up running and yoga and talked to his boss about some ongoing problems at work.

For the first month, they agreed that only when in private, Sophia would make a sexy whistle if she saw Raiz chewing his lip, to call it to his attention. Also, at the end of each day Raiz would tell Sophia about three times he consciously did not chew his lip, so she could celebrate it with him.

In her journal, Sophia vented to herself about how often she still caught him chewing and how ugly it looked. After two months, Raiz was able to stop chewing his lip (mostly), but Sophia kept supporting him for another year on engaging in practices to address his anxiety.

Example when partners' goals differ

Raiz wishes that Sophia would always be on time (or early) for events like he is. In fact, her frequent lateness, even when she's five minutes late, drives him crazy. He judges it as sloppiness and showing lack of respect.

Sophia, however, assesses herself as sufficiently punctual and does not particularly want to change this. So when they talk about this next it is Raiz' needs on the table, not hers.

Together they strategize about how to address his frustration: could he show up later? Bring a book? When they're meeting others, could he do a reality-check about whether they mind her minor lateness? Over time, Raiz becomes slightly more relaxed about punctuality and Sophia, no longer feeling judged, is more often right on time. But it continues to be an area of difference.

To summarize, the key to helping your partner change is to keep clear about whose needs are being addressed. You do this by (a) finding out what your partner does and doesn't wants to change, (b) committing to offer the type of support she finds effective, and only that type of support, and (c) vulnerably asking for help with your own feelings.

Healing the sources of pain

As therapists like to point out, our families of origin and our early life experiences greatly influence us, especially when it comes to how we cope in relationships. To get to the heart of conflicts, we often must delve into this more shadowy area, and do the personal work necessary to help ourselves (and our partners) heal from circumstances that have nothing to do with our current lives.

While many people choose to do healing work solely with skilled therapists, others choose to develop counseling skills to assist themselves, their friends, and their loved ones. We list a few resources for skill development at the end of this guide.

We hope that the example below, despite its brevity, will help illustrate what this healing might look like. Please note that the example is only offered for illustration, not to guide the inexperienced counselor.

We believe that healing early hurts is not only useful as "crisis" intervention, but as a valuable, perhaps necessary, component of supporting your relationship to be the best it can be.

Explore early hurts

Vonda was extremely upset that her partner Jon "ignored her" the night before at a friend's party. After talking about it for an hour (using the "finding win-win solutions" process previously described) they figured out some ways to feel more connected at social events. Then their conversation continued...

Jon: I'm so glad we've talked about this! I feel good about our solutions.

Vonda: Me, too. I'm very glad we eventually were able to listen to each other without being defensive.

Jon: I'm still wondering whether what happened tonight at the party might have been connected to something from your past. What do you think?

Vonda: (After thinking for a few minutes), You know, I didn't think of this before, but I'm remembering now how my father and my former husband acted at parties. Dad used to ignore my mom and flirt with other women, and Henry was always too caught up in "important" talks with other men to pay attention to me. Both of them made me feel worse than invisible. Just like I felt last night.

Jon: Ow. I bet that was painful, having two important men in your life ignore you that way. I'm sorry if the way I acted last night stirred up old wounds. Would you like to explore this a little more with me?

Vonda: Okay.

Jon: Can you remember a time, years ago, when your father upset you at a party? Try pretending for a moment that you're back in that situation, and this time you have total permission to tell your father exactly how you feel and how you want him to treat you. Don't worry about what would be right to say to him in reality. Just express yourself as honestly as you can. You can even pretend I'm your dad, if you want, but I won't respond as he would. I'll just encourage you to express your feelings.

Vonda: I'll try. But remember I'm not saying this to you, Jon, just to my Dad, back when I was ten years old. . . . "Dad, how dare you treat Mom like that! How dare you flirt with other women in front of her! I'm so embarrassed! And how come you pay so little attention to me when we're with other people. Don't you dare say I'm such a cute little girl and then ignore me, you jerk!"

Jon: Yes, tell me more!

(Vonda yells more at her pretend father, and then yells and cries with her pretend past husband. Jon keeps encouraging her to express her feelings.)

Vonda: Whew! I'm exhausted! And amazed you could listen to me for so long! I feel lighter, and clearer. I didn't realize that so much of what was making me mad last night came from earlier in my life. Thank you so much!

Re-evaluation co-counseling offers on-going classes, workshops, and publications to help lay people develop basic counseling skills. For many people seeking to address deep old wounds and patterns, peer counseling is best supplemented by professional therapy.

Commit to being allies

We not only have personal histories, but as social beings, we are very much affected by the conditions of the identity groups of which we are a part: male or female, gay or straight, Jewish or Gentile, etc. People are hurt in this society in many ways. Sometimes acknowledging larger societal patterns of oppression can help us, as individuals, realize that we are not personally responsible for some of the unconstructive behaviors we are caught in. Indeed, most of these behaviors and attitudes have been playing themselves out in the larger society long before we were born.

In addition to helping each other heal early personal hurts, partners can help each other heal by committing to being allies for each other across oppressed social identities (e.g. a man being an ally to a woman, or a white person being an ally to a person of color). Commit to being an ally to your partner even if you are not yet sure how to do it. You can learn how over time, both from your partner and from others who have worked to be allies across these differences.

> *Jon: You know, it seems to me what you experienced happens a lot between men and women. Men are taught to discount women, and women learn to feel powerless and invisible. I'm sorry for any ways that I may have learned to play into that hurtful male role. I want you to know that as a man I am committed to being your ally, and to doing whatever I can to support you as a woman to be powerful. I hope you'll teach me how I can be an ally for you.*

> *Vonda: No man ever said such a thing to me before! I can't tell you how much it touches me, especially after seeing men treat women badly all my life. Thank you, Jon.*

Re-evaluation co-counseling (in the "Resources" section) is good at explaining how societal oppression affects personal relationships, and offers support groups, workshops and journals specific to many identity groups.

Grow through compassion: key points

Use appreciation abundantly

> Notice everyday gifts
> Relieve tensions
> Relish similarities and differences
> Reinforce the positive
> Support personal growth
> Savor being together

Appreciations go deeper when you:

> Connect to the recipient as you speak
> Describe specifics, not positive judgments
> Disclose what's meaningful to you
> Empathize with the recipient
> Invite dialogue

Discover your partner's love language

> Words of affirmation
> Acts of service
> Receiving gifts
> Quality time
> Physical touch

> *- From Gary Chapman, The Five Love Languages*

Practice empathy

Understand what empathy is and isn't
Regularly ask for and offer empathy
Expect to try and try again
Mirror strong feelings

Help your partner change

Find out what your partner wants to change
Offer only the types of support they find effective
Get help for your own feelings

Design positive growth campaigns

Step 1: Make two lists
Ways you want to change
Ways you want your partner to change

Step 2: Choose your campaigns
Each choose one area where your lists overlap

Step 3: Carry out positive growth campaigns
Break your goal into small do-able steps
Lavish appreciation on every small step
Take frustrations elsewhere

Step 4: Discuss where your lists differ
See if any can become goals you hold together
If not, constructively handle your own reactions

Tips when you're trying to change

Start small
Strengthen your resolve to change
Break your goal into small steps
Bring friends into the campaign

Tips for supporting your partner to change

Appreciate every little step in the right direction
Help your partner appreciate their own successes
Take your negative feelings elsewhere
Know it takes time and persistence

Healing the sources of pain

Explore early hurts
  -listen to each other
  -distinguish the past from the present
  -learn counseling skills and/or see therapists

Commit to being allies across power differences
  -pledge to interrupt oppressive behavior
  -support your partner's empowerment

Chapter 4

Make decisions wisely

Chapter 4: Make decisions wisely

Couples make countless decisions together, some easy, but many tedious if not downright stressful. From the minor: "Shall we eat Italian or Chinese food tonight?" to the major: "Do we have kids together?" plus all the shades of importance in between: "Will we spend Easter with your family or Passover with mine?" The need for decision-making relentlessly permeates our adult lives.

Making decisions with ease adds to the sweetness and the security of being partnered with someone. In this section are some tools we developed after many struggles with less successful ways of making decisions together. We now use these effective decision-making methods every day.

Repetitive decisions

In ongoing relationships, certain decisions need to be made over and over, hundreds or thousands of times. As couples get clearer about their needs and preferences, such decision-making can become quicker and easier.

One of the ways that couples handle repetitive decisions is to **alternate turns.**

> *We'll see your family during summer holidays and my family in winter holidays.*

Another way is to **create role divisions.**
> *You pay the house bills each month. I'll handle our laundry.*

Another elegant short cut to repetitive decision-making we call **"rules of thumb."** These are useful in recurrent decisions where you want to choose freshly each time, yet where together you lack a clear preference or are ambivalent. Essentially, you agree in advance that the rule of thumb makes the decision for you. Then, if desired, you can still name any needs unmet by the decision and strategize how to meet them.

> *Shall we eat out tonight? Paulo has the slightest leaning towards eating out and Chris the slightest leaning to eat in. Their rule of thumb: "When in doubt, don't go out." They want eating out to remain special, not a habit, and to be conscious spenders.*
>
> *Chris: "Ok, since we have no clear combined preference, our rule of thumb is to eat in. Would you like to name what drew you to eat out?"*
>
> *Paulo: "I wanted some privacy from our housemates, plus I'm tired of cooking.*
>
> *Chris: "How about if I make dinner while you read alone. I'll bring it into our private work room and light a candle."*

You can deliberately use rules of thumb to nudge your relationship away from dulling habits and towards the direction of your deeper values. Here are idiosyncratic examples from our life:

> ***Should we keep working or rest?*** *Our rule of thumb: rest. It's so easy to be driven and keep working! Yet health is a strong value. Thanks to this rule of thumb, taking a 10-minute nap together has become a daily delight.*
>
> ***Shall we get into water (swim, shower, walk in the rain) or stay dry? Rule of thumb: Get wet.*** *We both feel instantly transformed by going in water, yet we're often resistant to each other's invitations. We're daunted by the hassle of changing clothes or by interrupting what we're doing. This rule of thumb inspires us to refresh ourselves more than we would otherwise.*
>
> ***Shall we make love or do something else? Our rule of thumb: make love.*** *Shifting into sexual energy sometimes sounds like more work than the satisfaction of handling our to-do lists or the relaxation of watching a movie. This rule of thumb helps us overcome reluctance and prioritize our sexual connection.*

Shall we ask each other for help or do it ourselves? Our rule of thumb: ask for help. When either of us feel burdened by the responsibilities of daily life, it can be hard to reach out. This rule of thumb reminds us not to assume the other is unavailable but instead ask for the support we want.

Tricky decisions

The following process for making decisions is the most thorough and useful one we've developed. At first glance, this process may seem cumbersome or complex. However, once you're fluent with the steps, it can be quick for most daily-life decisions and satisfyingly robust for the big ones. From the most minor decisions to the most difficult, following this can help your decision-making become straightforward, mutual, and even fun.

We call it the "Systematic Decision Making Process."

Systematic decision-making process

Step 1: Define the question.
Articulate a simple choice between two options.

Step 2: Name your leaning
- Do you lean towards one of the options?
- If yes, is your leaning slight, medium or strong?
- If it's a joint decision, combine your leanings together.
- If desired, explain why you have that leaning.

Step 3: Address concerns
- When you imagine choosing the option you lean towards, what concerns come up for you?
- What are a few creative ways to address those concerns?
- If desired, you can invite a listener's opinions.

Step 4: Make your decision
- What is your leaning now?
- Are you ready to make a decision?
- If not, repeat steps 2 and 3 until ready to decide.
- If yes, concisely summarize the decision made.

Step 5: Acknowledge lingering feelings
- Express any leftover feelings (e.g. regret, anxiety)
- Do not confuse expressing feelings with changing your mind.

To give a simple illustration, here is Chico helping Alison make a decision about what to do tonight. His role is to ask her the questions and to keep the process moving briskly.

> *A: Would you help me make a quick decision?*
> *C: Sure! What's the question?*
> *A: Shall I go to the movies tonight or stay home?*

Make sure the question is clear and simple. Work on just one question at a time.

> *C: What leaning do you have and how strong is it?*
> *A: I have a very slight leaning to go to the movies.*

Sometimes just calling this question cuts through a lot of ambivalence. It's fine for the person to say "no leaning" if she really has none. But don't let her sink into equivocating.

> *C: Why do you lean towards going?*
> *A: This is my one free night this week, and I really want to see the show playing down the street.*

Again, be sure the person sticks with why she has her leaning. Don't let her slip into why she's unsure. You may need to be assertive.

List all the concerns, without problem-solving yet.

C: Concerns to address?
A: Yeah. When am I going to get that report written, if not tonight? And I'm worried I'll be tired tomorrow since the show ends at 11pm.

Now the problem solving.

C: How could you meet those concerns? First, the report.
A: Well, I could change my meeting with Janet to next week and work Thursday night instead. And if she can't switch, I could work late after the meeting. That would work.
C: Good! How about your concern about being tired tomorrow?
A: Tomorrow I could nap before dinner and go to bed early.

Above, problem solving is straightforward, but often people need a lot of help to think up creative options and evaluate them.

C: What's your leaning now? Ready to make a decision?
A: Yes, I feel better about going. I'd like to call Janet about rescheduling our meeting, and then I'll ask Martha if she'll go with me to the nine o'clock show.
C: Great. Regrets?
A: I wish I had decided earlier so I could have made the seven o'clock show. And I wish you didn't have to work tonight so you could come with me!

To make joint decisions

Each person states a leaning. Then these are combined into a collective leaning.

Derek has a very strong leaning for option A and Janice has a medium leaning for option A. Collectively they have a strong leaning for option A. They follow the process and both participate.

Derek expresses a slight leaning for option B, while Janice names a slight leaning for option A. Collectively they thus have no leaning. They problem-solve together about both options, as described on the next page.

Derek has a slight leaning for option B but Janice has a strong leaning for option A, then collectively they have a slight leaning for option A. They then ask what concerns Derek would need to meet in order to go with the collective leaning.

Be aware of patterns in a relationship where one person typically states her preferences forcefully while the other understates his. In this case, you may need to compensate by weighing each person's expressed leaning differently, and in the long term, helping both to be equally assertive.

To make decisions when you have no leaning

If you truly have no leaning, then do problem solving quickly for both options. What concerns would you need to address in order to choose option A? What concerns would you address to meet in order to choose option B? Then check to see if a leaning has emerged. Usually one has.

When you're ambivalent

If you use the process and still feel terribly ambivalent, then probably something more is needed. Perhaps clarity will come after expressing strong feelings or from figuring out how the decision stirs up personal issues from your past. Perhaps you need to meditate and ask a deeper part of yourself what you need. Then come back to the process and see whether you are clearer. If fear is blocking you, it can help to frame the decision as between two fine options instead of between two bad (e.g., anxiety-provoking) options. Either one you choose is excellent! People who are burdened with habits of strong ambivalence can especially benefit from acknowledging that every decision comes with trade-offs and from using a clear process for decision-making.

Weighty decisions

Sometimes in relationships we face decisions that are complex, have high stakes, and/or are highly charged emotionally. A few examples: to have children or not, to move or change careers, to end a pregnancy, to adopt a child, to break up or divorce, or to undergo a risky medical procedure. Many scary and difficult decisions are part of relationship life.

The Systematic Decision-making Process described above can still be valuable when wrestling with weighty decisions, so long as you add several additional steps. It helps to have practiced the process many times with less important decisions.

Clarify the decision-maker(s)

Before Step 1, take extra care to clarify whether this is a joint decision, your decision, or your partner's. Think this through carefully. With many couple decisions, the decision must be made together. But some decisions need to be made or are better made by one person, even if the partner is strongly affected (for instance, whether to have a major medical procedure or choosing when to retire).

Clarify the weight of each person's input

Even if it is a joint decision, one of you may have more input than the other. Even if you decide something is your final decision, you must still decide how much weight to give your partner's input.

Vent emotional upset

If you're clogged with intense feelings, you won't be able to think clearly. Ask your partner or a friend you deeply trust (ideally, someone who is neither triggered by your decision nor directly affected by the outcome) to lovingly witness you for a specific amount of time while you express your feelings, such as grief, guilt, fear, and anger. Make it clear that his role is just to listen, not to fix the situation, offer opinions, or calm you down. Stick to your time agreement. Add this throughout the process as needed.

Elicit useful advice

If you have decided that this is your decision (namely, that your partner may give input but is not a co-decision-maker), you might need to do extra work to ensure your partner's input is constructive. After Step 3 where you name and address concerns, ask your partner first to empathize with your feelings and summarize the interests you have named. Ask your partner to give advice that directly addresses those interests, before your partner names and addresses his own values and interests. (If this is an emotionally challenging decision for the partner, they may need to get additional support elsewhere or even need to bow out of playing this tender role.)

Give time to sit with the decision

When you feel close to having made the decision, name a time frame to try on your decision before finalizing it. You might want to sit with it for hours, days, even weeks or months.

Practice communicating your decision

If you are making a decision you expect will be painful to your partner, practice how to be clean and clear about what you decided and why. Clearly communicate what you need to say to your partner.

To illustrate these additional steps of a weighty decision, we'll follow Yvette who has learned she has a late-stage cancer and is making the very difficult decision about how to respond.

Vent strong feelings: *Yvette asks her husband, Olivier, if he is open to listening to her grief, terror, and rage about having cancer. She also asks her women's group to give her space for these feelings and finds a therapist, so it is (hopefully) less of an emotional burden for Olivier.*

Clarify the decision-maker: *Yvette determines that she will make the decision herself about treatment, not have it be a joint decision with her husband. She gets input from her doctor and is also clear that it is not the doctor's decision.*

Clarify the weight of each person's input. *Yvette tells Olivier she will consider very seriously his feelings and thoughts, but at the end of the process, requests that he honor her wishes and let go of trying to influence her further.*

Elicit useful advice. *Yvette asks Olivier to tell her what he understood of her feelings, core values and hopes, after he has listened awhile. Yvette asks him to then give advice that is based on those understandings as fully as he can. Then she asks him to state his feelings, values, and hopes and to offer his own input.*

Give time to sit with the decision. *After a month of research, weighing options and getting her loved one's input, Yvette makes a tentative decision but still feels terrified. So she decides to give herself another 48 hours to sit with that leaning and pray about it before finalizing the decision.*

Practice communicating the decision. *Yvette role-plays in her women's group telling Olivier that she has decided (against her doctor's advice) that for the next 3 months she will only do alternative treatments. She requests that he share his fear and grief with her, but then take those feelings to other friends for support. Yvette requests Olivier join her for a 15-minute daily prayer time for both of them.*

Decisions as complex and emotionally charged as these can be extremely challenging even with the best tool kit. By practicing the systematic decision-making process for your daily decisions, you can become skillful enough to lean on it for the whammy decisions life brings.

Agreement-check

Whenever you've made a decision together, whether major or minor, take a few moments to be sure you're actually on the same page. Couples often feel frustrated when one person thought the other had agreed to something, yet the other remembered it differently or didn't even think it was a decision.

> *Sorry, I thought 10am was just a rough time for us to start work together. I didn't think it mattered if I arrived 15 minutes later.*

> *You wanted to be the one to call your mom? I thought we said whoever could get to it first was fine.*

> *You thought I was going to buy the plane tickets? I thought you were going to!*

This glitch may not be a problem of poor memory, but rather of not taking the time to carefully check that a) you both are consciously making an agreement, and b) you are agreeing to the same thing.

We designed the following ritual as a way to be sure we're on the same page.

Ritual to check agreements

Step 1: Confirm you're both ready to make an agreement.
Step 2: Summarize it.
Step 3: Verbally check for agreement.
Step 4: Signal physically to affirm the agreement.

> *Angel: Seems like we're ready to decide to go away for the weekend? Is that right?*
>
> *Murielle: Yes! We've agreed to drive off on Friday between 7 and 7:30pm and get home sometime (to be decided later) Sunday afternoon. Is that's what we're deciding?*
>
> *Both: Yes!*
> *Both: High five!! (They clap hands)*

Make decisions wisely: key points

Streamlined repetitive decisions

Alternate turns
Create role divisions
Make "rules of thumb"

The Systematic Decision-Making Process

Step 1: Define the question between two choices
Step 2: Name your leaning
Step 3: Address concerns
Step 4: Make your decision
Step 5: Acknowledge lingering feelings

For weighty decisions

Add these steps to the Systematic Decision-Making:
Vent emotional upset
Clarify the decision-maker(s)
Decide the weight of each person's input
Elicit useful advice
Give time to sit with the decision
Practice communicating the decision

Ritual to check agreements

Confirm you're both ready to make an agreement
Summarize what has been agreed upon
Check for agreement verbally and nonverbally

Chapter 5

Hot topics

Chapter 5: Hot topics

When we wrote the first version of this guide, we were overwhelmed as new parents to our son, and still raw from the stillbirth of our daughter the previous year. We had barely begun our careers and were less familiar with the stresses that work brings to relationship. The challenges of middle age weren't even on our minds.

Now that we're pushing 60, we have updated this guide with some of what we've learned and invented in the intervening years, especially ideas and tools related to the "hot topics" that follow. As we mentioned in the introduction, we're not trying to be comprehensive about any of these five topics. There are many books and training programs in each of these areas that go into much greater depth. We're only seeking to share a little of what's been helpful to us, hoping some of it might also be helpful to you.

Sexuality

For many couples, sex is easy and exciting at the start of their relationship, but as life pressures increase, and as years and decades go by, sex may become increasingly stale, sparse, or even non-existent. Although our culture is more open than it used to be around sexuality, it is still private and vulnerable territory for many of us, with few opportunities for exchange or guidance. Many have had a relationship to sexuality that is unhealthy or worse: inhibited, compulsive, and sometimes even abusive. We make no claim to have great expertise in this area, but we have worked on it. Below are some of the practices and resources that are making a difference for us currently, as we explore how to savor greater sexual connectedness even as our sexual energy wanes.

Make sexual dates

Many of us acquired the mis- conception (perhaps from seeing movies where ecstatic couples tear off each other's clothes) that in order to be genuine, lovemaking should just happen spontaneously as we feel swept up in desire. But for many couples over 40, for those exhausted from kids and/or demanding jobs, or for those who have been together a long time, that type of desire may happen rarely. If you rely on spontaneous  combustion, being sexual together is likely to be less and less frequent. Making sexual dates keeps sex in your life.

At first, planning a specific time for sex may seem unbearably contrived. You might think, "If my partner needs to schedule time for sex, then they don't really desire me!" Or it may seem like pressure: "I can't get aroused on demand!" Or too vulnerable to suggest: "What if I'm now refused—again!" The sections below address some of these concerns.

Say yes...and then negotiate

Here's our rule: all invitations for sex dates are answered with a "yes," although the time can be negotiated. This rule provides active encouragement for invitations and removes the fear of rejection.

Decide what type of date

A sexual date is simply an invitation to give and receive intimate pleasure. Within that broad definition many kinds of connection are possible. Talk together about what kind of date you'll have, either when you're scheduling the date or when your date starts.

If you feel awkward or embarrassed talking about sex (as many do), deciding what sexual date to have offers great practice to be better able to discern and articulate what you truly want. Here are some possibilities to get you started, taken from the books *Hot Monogamy* and *Expanded Orgasm* listed in the Resources section.

Sensual: Deliberately keep genital touching and orgasm off limits. You can still get aroused, but the focus is on giving and receiving sensual pleasure.

The usual: Make love in whatever ways are most comfortable and easy for both of you, without them needing to be creative or special. Relax and enjoy.

Leisurely: Set aside twice or three times as much time as you usually take for lovemaking. What you do might not be much different, but the feeling will be more spacious.

Quickie: You may sometimes enjoy something short and sweet when the energy is there, or just necessarily brief due to lack of more time. Sometimes you might decide to offer one-way attention to the person who gets most easily aroused or the one who most craves the attention at that time.

Adventurous: Select together something you rarely or never do, and give it a try. See the book Hot Monogamy for a list of possibilities.

Purposeful: Experiment with exercises to help you overcome stuck or awkward places in your sexual connection. During "sexercises," partners often give and receive feedback more intentionally than in usual lovemaking. Sexercises take work (although the work can be fun). The books in the resource section offer many sexual exercises. See also "Feedback" section below.

Take time to transition

Artists and athletes know that warm-ups are essential to performance. For instance, a singer might take 30 minutes to stretch her body and do gentle vocal scales before singing.

Good lovemaking comes from being in your body, present in the moment, emotionally open, and connected to your partner. It's a far cry from how many of us spend our days: sitting at the computer or doing other body-stressing activities, rushing through lists of things to do, feeling pressured, and disregarding our feelings.

Figure out what helps each of you transition into a state conducive to lovemaking. Your ways of transitioning could be quite different for each of you. If you're having a pre-planned sex date, decide whether to include transition time in your sex dates, or agree that you'll each take transition time before your date starts. Consider these components:

> *Body: What helps you connect to your body in a good way? A hot shower... stretching... mild exercise... massage... a nap... Avoid your e-mail!*

> *Mind: What helps you let go of preoccupations? Talking about them... writing a list for later... handling one last thing... prayer... meditation...*

> *Emotion: What does your heart need to feel peaceful and open? Journal-writing... listening... emotional release through tears or laughter...*

> *Environment: What's nourishing to you? Candles...beauty... music... comfort... privacy...*

Give and receive feedback

The idea that we should psychically "just know" how to please our partner is a damaging myth. While some couples do have powerful sexual attraction or "good chemistry," other couples don't. Even when couples enjoy great sexual chemistry, sex is a set of skills that improve with practice. Yet, while making love, many shy away from giving and receiving feedback, feeling awkward or simply fearing to interrupt the flow. We recommend finding low-stress times to talk about sex, and developing a toolkit of exercises to help facilitate connection and communication.

Agree on a feedback time

Decide on a particular date ahead of time to experiment with giving and receiving feedback. The goal here is simply to improve your communication or to work on some edge for either of you, not fabulous lovemaking per se.

Remember that every moment is fresh

For many people, especially women, what they find arousing changes from moment to moment. What "works" one time won't necessarily work the next. So the goal is not to memorize rules or patterns of what's arousing, but rather to become adept at reading your partner's subtle (or not so subtle) cues, and to become relaxed at giving and receiving feedback in the moment.

Mix appreciation and encouragement with requests

Notice and tell your partner when something feels good. "Mmm, I like your tongue there!" Then make one very specific simple request in a relaxed voice. "Lighter." Then affirm that change before making another one "Mmmm, better! Could you do the same thing even lighter?" That makes two appreciations for every request.

For more feedback ideas see the books *Expanded Orgasm* and *The ESO Program*, in the Resources section at the end.

Find language you both like

Much of the language for sexual acts and body parts can sound either crass or clinical. Play around together and choose or create words you both enjoy.

For example, we have made up names for four kinds of touch: "earth touches" (firm massage or compression), "water touches" (smooth and flowing), "air touches" (light and tingling), "fire touches" (with intent to arouse). What new language might be helpful to you and your partner?

Make up simple exercises or games

Some people find it hard to know or describe what feels good or what they want. Creating games that offer very simple choices can make this more fun and easy. Here are some simple games that we came up with:

Variation game

Partner A is arousing Partner B in a specific way. Partner A then asks: "Which of these three variations do you like best? Here's #1... now #2.... now #3....."

Partner A tries to make each variation distinct and to do each for at least a minute. (Of course, B might be getting increasingly aroused through the sequence, so it's not exactly a scientific test!) Partner A might even put into words exactly what A's doing each time before she does it, so B can better picture what A is doing.

B aims to relax and enjoy. B feels free to say, "Do that one again" or "Move on to the next one." After B has experienced all three, B tries to describe not only which B preferred but why. Remember that this is just a preference of the moment, not for all time.

Options game

Partner C verbally offers three distinctly different lovemaking activities that involve arousing Partner D: "Would you rather I do this... or this... or this?" They must all be things that genuinely appeal to C to do.

D then chooses one and C does it. If C requests it, D can try to explain why, or say his response to each of the offers. (D: "They all appeal, but I think I'd need to be more aroused before experiencing #1 and #3.)

Then switch roles.

Theme game

Together they choose a theme. The theme provides a focus or limit for each partner during this time of lovemaking. Then they talk afterwards about what each enjoyed (or didn't enjoy) about that theme. Some examples of themes:

- One of you keeps eyes closed the whole time.
- Maintain much more (or much less) eye contact than usual.
- Kiss much more (or much less) than you usually do.
- One of you is dressed and the other naked.

Try "OM-ing"

"OM" stands for Orgasmic Meditation, a specific practice of giving 15-minutes of one-way, genital touching, usually to a woman, a term coined by Nicole Daedone written in her book *Slow Sex*. This deceptively simple practice has been powerful for many couples, in part because it creates a safe practice that even very busy people can invest in, one where the recipient can release performance anxiety and relax into receiving sexual attention. It often untangles the mystery, embarrassment, and confusion that can surround female arousal, and partners learn a great deal about giving and receiving feedback.

Work with yin and yang energies

Traditional Chinese Taoist philosophy speaks of the complementary duality of yin and yang, both essential for wholeness. Yin is associated with softness, yielding, the moon, nighttime, and femininity. Yang is associated with hardness, forcefulness, the sun, daytime, and masculinity.

The difference between yin and yang energies can supply dynamic energy to sexual connection. Every person has yang ("masculine") energy and traits, as well as yin ("feminine") traits in different proportions. It helps to know and accept which type of energy is more natural to each partner and which is a turn-on. In both heterosexual and in same-sex relationships, couples can be fed by expanding and savoring these differences rather than by reducing or denying them.

In the past generation, as a result of the feminist, gay rights, and queer movements, gender roles have become less rigid. Much of that has helped create healthier relationships between men and women (e.g. it has helped men be more receptive and women more powerful, and increased both women and men's sense of wholeness). However, feminist men sometimes confuse the wonderful commitment to be non-sexist with unnecessarily holding back (or letting atrophy) their potent, sexy yang energy. Feminist women sometimes confuse being powerful with unnecessarily denying their receptive, sexy yin energy.

Sex writer David Deida's controversial books speak eloquently to the interplay of yin and yang. Yin partners can be like the ocean, buffeted by ever-changing emotions. They want their passionate, fluid feelings to be welcomed in a non-reactive way. At the same time, they long to be held steady by the strong directionality of their yang partners, to be "penetrated by their love" both figuratively and literally.

Often, yin partners need to feel emotionally close before they can open up sexually, while yang partners need sexual connection first in order to open up emotionally. This difference alone has caused many couples to stalemate. Instead, partners can begin lovemaking by taking turns giving each other attention for 5-10 minutes. The yin partner can first receive cuddling and empathetic listening... perhaps a chance to cry... then the yang partner can receive whatever sexual attention the yin partner now feels ready to give. After full lovemaking the yang partner might be more receptive to receiving emotional attention.

Expect difficult emotions

Many people have experienced some form of sexual abuse and need years of personal growth and/or therapy to heal from that legacy. But even for people with no traumatic history, difficult feelings can arise during lovemaking: fear, sorrow, shame, loneliness, guilt, or anger... feelings that may be completely unrelated to the present moment or relationship. Learn how to help each other safely explore and release those feelings without taking them personally. Below are just a few of the many sexual topics where irrational feelings are bound to arise. See also "Healing the sources of pain" section earlier in this guide.

Feelings about different desire levels

Many of us have a history of feeling either pressured to have sex or rejected for wanting sex (or both) and we can easily fall into our familiar pattern. For the partner who wants less sex, feeling pressured or obligated can erase genuine desire; for the one who wants more, feeling needy or rejected can generate resentment and withdrawal. This can be great territory for playing with the "role reversals" described earlier in this guide. For instance, if your partner has a history of being rejected for wanting sex, set up a role reversal where you ask your partner to make love, who vociferously refuses you again and again. You might both laugh a lot.

Feelings about different turn-ons

If one of you feels uncomfortable with a proposed sexual activity, instead of assuming that territory is off limits, can you welcome the feelings? Set aside time separate from lovemaking to explore them. Take turns as speaker and listener. Encourage the person to express and even exaggerate their negative reactions (e.g., "Yuck! Gross! I would NEVER do that!"). Listener, take nothing personally! Explore the roots of both desire and repulsion. After some tears or laughter, you might be able to more easily find some common ground.

Feelings about aging

Sexual energy often declines with aging and brings new relationship challenges. We address this in the "Aging" section.

Feelings about fertility

Especially for people who have had childbearing issues (such as trouble conceiving, abortions, miscarriages or stillbirths, or more or fewer children than they wish for) having sex can bring unbidden emotions, even years and decades later. Don't be surprised. Allow room for the feelings.

A related aside: For the two of us, "Fertility Awareness" was a wonderful way to both prevent and assist conception. It was our primary form of birth control for three decades. We highly recommend it for couples who communicate well and have the discipline to adhere conscientiously 100% to the key principles. See resource section for more information.

Make agreements about exclusiveness

Most of us were raised with the assumption that monogamy is the right and only way to show committed love. Many consider adultery a sin. Even for those who don't have religious views on this, many believe that if someone in the couple "cheats" and the "ugly truth" comes out, that's likely the end of the relationship.

OK, here we have views that may be troublesome to some readers. We respect that people have different values. Personally, however, we are pained to witness how the strict and emotionally volatile belief that monogamy is the only option for stable relationships has brought suffering to incalculable numbers of people. Pure monogamy works beautifully for some couples. But evidently it does not for a great many others, including many couples that espouse it.

Exclusiveness means different things for different people. For some people just thinking sexual thoughts or being close friends with another person other than your partner is threatening. Others have more relaxed boundaries, and many aren't sure what their boundaries are until they get crossed. As with everything in this guide, our strong bias is towards partners practicing honest communication. Through skillful and compassionate listening to get at each partner's underlying needs, you can creatively negotiate agreements rather than assume hard and fast rules.

This kind of openness is very different from the secret intimacies many couples maintain. Even though hidden relationships sometimes "work" (e.g. we know one loving marriage that survived for 50 years in part because one partner had a long-term "secret" lover), for us, keeping secrets is a violation of the trust that underlies deep closeness. We endorse openness and trust, not secrecy.

Even in subcultures where people are open to exploring non-monogamous arrangements, pulling off respectful "open relationships" is a considerable feat. As a practice it demands an extraordinary level of personal self-awareness, communication skill, sensitivity to others, and willingness to process what comes up for everyone. We're humbled by how much work open non-monogamy takes to do well, as we both experienced in our early 20s and have seen over the years from friends who are committed to open or poly-amorous relationships.

Below are two different real-life examples of people happy in unconventional and non-exclusive relationships. The names have been changed to protect privacy.

Izzy and Jules have been happily married and mostly monogamous for 30 years. There is one exception: once or twice a year, Izzy spends the weekend with a lover, a woman he was involved with before he met Jules. Despite some awkwardness about it in the early years of their marriage, this has been a remarkably stress-free arrangement. The woman, too, is in a solid marriage with good communication, and her husband is similarly unthreatened by this sexual connection. The energy between the lovers primarily is one of friendship, not an ongoing romantic preoccupation that could easily stir jealousy.

Tiffany and Beth savored ten years of a devoted monogamous relationship. Then, over the next ten years, they gradually added Paula to their lives as a second sexual partner for Tiffany and as a close friend for Beth. All three now co-parent the children and are accepted as a committed threesome by their in-laws. (In their professional lives they are "out" about being gay but not "out" about their non-monogamy.) To achieve this stable, happy and unconventional state has taken hundreds of hours of skillful processing and careful agreement setting. Because all three of them view pol-yamory as part of their life's work as agents of cultural change, they do not resent the investment it has required.

If you are drawn to venture into open, non-monogamous terri-tory—even to nonsexual, intimate relationships that could be threatening to your partner—here are a few of our suggestions:

Attend first to your primary relationship. Make sure you are not using other relationships as an "easy" way to get around areas of discontent in your primary relationship. Deal with those first and foremost directly in your primary relationship.

Talk about non-sexual closeness. Discuss with your partner how you both feel about non-sexual yet intimate relationships with other friends. Consider different types of situations, as well as how you feel about closeness to people of each gender. For example, how do you each feel about: friendly snuggling, intense dancing, frequent texting, long phone conversations, trips that include over-night stays…. when the primary partner is present… or absent? Know that predicting reactions in theory may be quite different from what happens in reality.

Listen in turns. Be sure to leave plenty of room for each of you to express your feelings. Take turns listening. Listen some more. Explore what needs (e.g., for security, trust, communication, ad-venture, companionship) underlie the feelings and discuss creative ways to meet important needs, either within the relationship, or with others. Decide what you're both willing to try out.

Expect many conversations. Expect to have these conversations many times, as needs, feelings, and situations change.

Be discreet. If you choose to be sexually non-monogamous, be thoughtful about discussing your choices with others. Most people have strong beliefs and feelings about this and passionately disap-prove of (or feel threatened by) alternative arrangements. Don't expect all your friends and family to support your experiments.

Find allies. On the other hand, do find support. Others have walked the road of open relationships and you can learn from friends, local support groups, books, or online research.

Keep agreements. Above all, negotiate clear agreements. Scrupulously uphold all decisions you make together in order to maintain each other's trust, and evaluate and revise these agreements as often as needed.

Sexuality: key points

Make sexual dates

> Say yes…then negotiate when and what
> Decide what type of date

Take time to transition

> Decide if transition time is solo or together
> Attend to body, mind, emotion, and environment

Give and receive feedback

> Agree on a feedback time
> Remember that every moment is fresh
> Mix requests with encouragement
> Find language you both like
> Make up simple exercises or games
> Try "OM-ing"

Work with yin and yang energies

Celebrate and play with the differences
Men can be strongly yang and still non-sexist
Women can be deeply yin and still empowered

Creatively address the needs of both energies
Yin opens to sex after emotional closeness
Yang opens to emotional closeness after sex

Expect difficult feelings

Old feelings often arise in sex about issues like
- desire levels
- turn-ons and turn-offs
- aging
- fertility

Don't take feelings personally. Take turns. Empathize.

Make agreements about exclusivity

Attend first to your primary relationship
Discuss non-sexual closeness
Listen in turns
Expect many conversations
Be discreet
Find allies
Keep agreements

Money

According to a report on CNBC, 90% of marriage break ups are because of money. Need we say more?

The two of us have been incredibly lucky to have had ample financial slack throughout our years together. So we can't speak personally to the lack-of-money stress that wracks (and wrecks) many couples. Nonetheless, it's taken work to blend our different money backgrounds, values, and styles. All the skills described earlier—taking turns, empathizing, being clear whose needs are on the table—have made a huge difference when tackling this touchy subject.

You can find thousands of helpful books and websites about money management in general; below are just a few of the specific money-related concepts and tools that helped us as a couple.

By the way: our profession for 30 years was promoting conversations about money and values. See *More than Money Journal* in the resource section to access a treasure trove of 43 free back issues of money stories and wisdom.

Exchange money histories

For many people, money carries a complex and emotionally charged history. It can feel vulnerable simply to talk about money, much less to actually share finances. Money easily brings up feelings of power and powerlessness, of judgment and fear of judgment.

Early in a serious relationship, before starting to share money, we recommend taking time to tell each other your money histories. Since there's often so much to tell, you might do it over several sessions, with each of you sharing on a particular topic (e.g., your parents' and grandparents' financial and class situations… positive and negative money messages from your family of origin… how you related to money as a child, as a teenager, and as a young

91

adult… your work history… areas of financial competence and incompetence, where you feel pride and shame, confusion and clarity… how you handled money in previous relationships… your experiences and values in earning, spending, saving, and giving…). If the conversation becomes emotionally intense, take short turns, rotating between talking and listening to your partner. Be sure to empathize with your partner's feelings before asking questions or tackling differences. By taking the time for these conversations, you'll be in much better shape to join your financial futures, as you'll both be more aware of each other's strengths and challenges.

Building on what you've learned from exchanging money histories, each of you try to name both the strengths and limitations of your own money style. Then discuss how each person's distinct strengths might serve your collective financial lives, and how you might use each other to shore up your individual weaknesses.

> *Preston's nuclear family struggled for basic necessities, while Derrick grew up with relative abundance. Not surprisingly, they developed very different money styles. Over time, they learned to appreciate that Preston's experience led him to be a thorough and careful money-manager, something that has greatly benefitted the couple's joint life. He has helped Derrick understand key financial concepts and make more thoughtful choices. And Derrick's more relaxed attitude about money has helped Preston enjoy the money they share without habitual anxiety.*

Address differences in power

This article of ours and cartoon by Johnny Lapham are adapted from "Balance of Power," in *More than Money Journal, issue #5.*

Many couples strive for a sense of equality and balance in their intimate relationships. They hunger for partnerships where both people feel powerful: able to get what they want in the relationship and in their own lives.

Large money differences often upset this dream of equality. The one with greater income or assets in a couple is frequently perceived by both parties as having more power: more influence over the couple's decisions, more freedom to craft his or her own life, and more authority to decide whether and how the couple will share financial resources.

In other areas of life, the rules of social interaction usually cushion people from confronting economic differences directly. For example, people may work side-by-side with others earning twenty times more or less than they do, but they don't ask their co-workers, "How do you feel about our difference in pay?" Couples who cross social or economic strata in their intimate relationships eventually confront these painful questions. They are challenged to meet economic differences head on, opening their hearts as well as minds.

For many people, financial differences and power imbalances are hard to untangle because they are so emotionally charged. Here are a few of the complex feelings people struggle with:

For those with less money:

> *I'm embarrassed to even bring up the subject of money. I'd hate for her to think I'm greedy or out for her money. Besides, it's hers.*

> *I resent having to be the one to bring this up. If Howard trusted me, he would just treat the money as ours.*

> *I'm scared to assume responsibility for Fred's money. He grew up learning to manage it, and I was taught nothing about it.*

For those with more money:

> *I feel ashamed that I've barely taken control of my money. I'm afraid if I share my money with Peter he'll be just like my dad, either mocking me or taking over.*

> *I'm scared to share money with Joan because I'm not convinced she's completely committed to us being together. But the problem is circular: it seems her discomfort with our money differences makes it hard for her to commit.*

> *I feel critical of how Jonathan uses money, and so don't want to share what I have. I don't know what to do about my judgments.*

Some couples try to tiptoe around their power differences, fearing that talking about them will open a "Pandora's Box" of unsolvable issues. But differences left unaddressed often deepen into chilly reservoirs of distance and mistrust. On the other hand, with persistent work (done gently and respectfully), even complicated and emotionally charged imbalances often can be untangled and resolved over time.

If you and your partner are trying to reduce your money-related power differences, you might find yourself working through the following steps:

Step 1: Voice discontents. Most often, one of you will start to voice (sometimes indirectly) frustration with the power dynamics in the relationship. Soon both of you are unhappy with the economic arrangements. Even if neither of you feel ready yet to change your arrangements or know what to do yet, this uncomfortable stage is actually an important first step towards greater balance.

Step 2: Recognize societal influences. Part of the healing process is to notice how the relationship is influenced by dynamics from the wider society. Your challenges are not just personal. Financial differences are often complicated by experiences of societal discrimination (or privilege) due to gender, race, class, age, disability, religion, etc. For instance, compared to a partner from a "dominant" group (e.g., male, white, upper-class) a partner from a "subordinate" group is likely to have less earning power, less credibility competing for higher status jobs, and less self-confidence about his or her power in the world. It's important to unpack the societal as well as family baggage so people can be sensitive to what is likely to be potentially painful or even traumatic to the other, and to explore how to be helpful.

These social differences may exacerbate financial inequalities (for instance, when an upper-class white person is building a relationship with a working-class person of color) or create confusing crosscurrents (for instance, when someone who is wealthy and young is with someone who is older and working-class).

Step 3: Dialogue. Take the time and establish the trust to talk directly about how you each experience the money and power differences in the relationship. Use the skills described earlier in this guide: taking turns, empathizing, knowing whose needs are on the table. Explore the effects of dominant and subordinate roles on your relationship to money. Seek support of others from your own background to grow in awareness and heal from the past.

Ask each other what has been good and what has been hard about being from your own class backgrounds, and listen deeply to each other's stories. Affirm your commitment to be together and validate the important qualities you each bring, despite your differences, to the relationship and to your lives.

Step 4: Explore options. Once both of you feel that your differing life histories have been heard and respected, you can more constructively discuss the nitty-gritty of what you want financially. Don't hesitate to get technical and emotional support from friends and financial professionals. Aim to generate a range of possible options that could move your financial relationship in directions you want to go.

Step 5: Experiment and evaluate. Choose among the various options and come up with creative ways to move towards balancing financial power in manageable steps. (See "Four aspects of financial sharing" below.) After a designated time of implementation, discuss how well your experiments are meeting your goals and revise them as needed.

Decide what to share

Many people assume that if they've "become a couple" they should share money 100%, and if they don't, there must be something wrong with the relationship. In reality, there are numerous creative, compatible ways in which couples can both share and keep separate their financial lives.

We've found it helpful to name four different aspects of financial sharing, to discuss each of them separately, and to know that any arrangements made can shift over time. In none of these four areas does sharing need to be "all or nothing."

Sharing expenses: This is usually the first area to arise, as couples figure out who pays for what and why. Negotiations sometimes start on the first date. There's no rule that says couples must split shared expenses 50-50, or must split all types of expenses the same. All sorts of variations can work as long as agreements are mutual, clear, followed, and regularly evaluated as needs change.

Sharing day-to-day management: Whoever takes on more of the daily money management (i.e. paying the bills, handling banking and investing, writing checks to charity, taking care of taxes, etc.) often experiences greater financial clarity and influence. If most or all daily money management is handled by one partner, you can help balance the power by having regular check-ins, perhaps every 1-4 months, to be sure the less-involved partner fully understands what's being done and why.

Sharing decision-making: Decision-making about money can be separate from legal ownership. For instance, you could pool your savings into one account to put into investments, but decide that one partner will be making all the investment decisions. Or you could decide to make charitable decisions together, even though the accounts you each donate from are legally separate and you have different amounts of money in them.

Even if you keep your day-to-day financial decision-making separate, your life together is hugely affected by the values that guide your long-term money decisions. What ultimately is the money for? How much do you need to feel secure? If you have or anticipate financial surplus, how will you decide what to do with it? These big decisions can be shared or not. Even if a pre-nuptial agreement keeps your assets legally separate, you can choose to give each other decision-making influence over actions related to your money—or not.

Sharing ownership: If you have sufficient trust between you, you might legally transfer money to joint ownership, whether or not you are legally married. Sharing financial ownership can happen quickly, over time, or not at all. Even if you never share ownership over your money, you can still share expenses, decision-making and/or money management.

Make written plans together

How do you know if you're on the same page about money? Few things have helped us as much as creating written plans together: spending plans, a lifetime financial plan, a multi-year giving plan, and an estate plan or will. Even though the pressures of daily life make it difficult to carve out time for these important but not-urgent plans, the returns can be enormous: greater peace of mind and ability work out differences.

We believe that the clarity these plans can give you over the long haul as a couple will make them well worth their time and effort. You can spread the work out over time – for instance, have a goal of making one type of plan per year for the next four years.

Enjoy the process! Like so much in this guide, the act of creating these plans will help you articulate your values more clearly to yourself and build into your relationship a foundation of listening, openness and trust.

Spending plan

Whether you live on a budget or just spend as you please, tracking your expenses and then reflecting together on your separate or joint spending can be an illuminating values-clarification exercise as a couple. Even doing it for just a month or two can be useful.

> *For years, Roberto and Zack met in January to review their income and expenses of the past year and to evaluate how well their spending matched their values. They didn't need or want to live on a budget, but did appreciate this simple way to keep moving their spending choices in the direction of their values. Last year, they decided to eat out less and instead to use the money they saved to buy special groceries at Whole Foods and Trader Joe's. They also set a goal of doubling what they spend on gifts for friends.*

Long-term financial plan

How much money do you actually need, individually and collectively, to feel secure long-term? How much can you feel free to spend? On what do you plan to spend it?

Making a long-term financial plan will give you both a much better picture of how much money you'll need for basic expenses and how much discretionary spending you can afford. You can make one plan for your joint lives or each have your own plan if most of your money is separate.

If this seems daunting, here are a few suggestions:

Use the help of a fee-only certified financial planner. The planner can help you create an initial plan, or if you are reasonably confident on the computer, you can draft a plan yourself on financial planning/retirement planning software and then have a professional planner check your work. Having a financial plan on your own computer (instead of just the planner's computer) will enable you to play with parameters, try on different scenarios, and easily change your plan over time.

Value the planning process. Perhaps making a joint plan will be quick and easy for you. But don't be surprised if it raises feelings of anxiety, confusion, and values differences between you. Take the time you need to do it thoroughly and get to the bottom of what is important to both of you, but keep the process moving to completion.

Expect to revise your financial plan every few years, when major changes happen in your lives or in the economy. Any plan is simply a good guess. Then reality happens!

Giving plan

Couples sometimes have very different beliefs and practices about giving, both the amounts to give and where the money should go. Should your "surplus" be put towards savings or towards giving? Should some level of giving continue no matter what your financial circumstances are? What causes do you each care about and why? What about gifts to family and friends in need? These questions can engender strong feelings and opinions. As we suggest in the "Money histories" section, take time to thoroughly hear each other out, including the history of your values and beliefs, before trying to craft solutions.

Whether you decide to jointly make all of your giving choices, or to do some or all of your giving separately, we encourage you to work out multi-year, written giving plans. Include how much you intend to give per year (as a dollar amount, or percentage of income or assets), the methods and timing of your gifts, and the kinds of organizations or causes you want to support. You might include a "discretionary fund" of an amount for the year that you can each give spontaneously to things that move you (e.g. friends' pet projects, walk-a-thons, etc.).

Working together on your giving plans will not only help prevent future conflicts, but will help each of you be more conscious, effective, and satisfied in whatever giving you do.

Estate plan or will

If you don't have a will yet, either as individuals or as a couple, make one this week! Any will is better than none. Just sit and write a letter as if you were writing to a friend. Lawyers can then make it official. If your situation is simple enough, you can even just use an online template and get it notarized. You can always improve it, but get it done!

To whom do you want to leave your possessions …your financial assets? Remember, a will is written for the possibility that you might die tomorrow. You're not guessing about the future; you're making important decisions about your finances right now. It is a wonderful values clarification exercise for couples at any stage of being together. How much money will you leave to your children? Will any of your assets go to charity? You can learn a great deal about each other by talking through the many values questions involved in creating your wills.

Once the legal part is complete, you might write personal notes to loved ones explaining the thinking behind your decisions and expressing your love. These more informal letters can be referenced in your will or just filed where your executor (the person you name to implement the will) can find them.

Money: key points

Exchange money histories

Plan on several sessions
Explore many topics (in childhood, youth, adulthood)
Take turns and empathize
Discuss ways to build on strengths
Discuss ways to address limitations

Address differences in power

Voice discontents
Recognize societal influences
Dialogue
Explore options
Experiment and evaluate

Four ways to share money

Discuss whether and how to share:
    Expenses
    Management
    Decision-making
    Ownership
Sharing money is not all or nothing.

Make written plans together

Spending plan
Long-term financial plan
Giving plan
Estate plan or will

Parenting

How do most couples get along once they add all the intense demands of parenting? For ourselves, we relied heavily on all the skills described in the first section of this guide. Good thing we had nearly a decade to practice them before getting pregnant!

Throughout much of our son's early years, Christopher struggled with fathering and Anne struggled to affirm Christopher's contributions rather than add to his already ample self-criticism. The concepts and skills described in "Helping each other change" truly saved our relationship. The practice of slathering on praise as described above in the "Appreciations" section was essential in the early years and continues to give us nourishment now, as we parent our young adult son.

Below are a few of the additional skills and insights that helped us through the journey of parenting.

Learn from role models

We learn a lot, consciously and unconsciously, by what we absorb of others' behavior. Take the time to discuss with your partner other couples you know as parents, to see what you can learn. It's great to do this kind of sharing at different stages of parenting (e.g., before you conceive, when children are small, when they are teens, and when they are young adults). Here are some exercises we found particularly helpful:

Exercise: Reflect on your parents' relationship
Share each of your observations of your own parents' relationship and how parenting seemed to affect them as a couple. Talk about how you experienced their relationship as a child and how you feel about it now. What would you wish to emulate in their relationship as parents and what would you like to do differently? What assumptions have you internalized about how couples parent together from the ways your parents behaved?

Exercise: Reflect on other couples' parenting
Name other couples you know you (including peers, friends of
your parents, relatives) who parent together and whose relationships inspire you. Discuss what you would like to emulate as well
as ways you would differ.

Negotiate big decisions

There are various big decisions about parenting. Probably the first
one, the decision whether or not to have a child, is one of the big-
gest decisions many couples face. Although some people say "just
go ahead and do it," if the two of you have fundamentally different
expectations about parenting, these are likely to come back and bite
you in the years ahead when you'll have little slack to talk them over.

Talk before you act. If your conversations uncover big differences,
don't give up. Use the tools in this guide, especially the systematic
decision-making model, to think creatively and negotiate how to
maximize meeting different needs. Even when the needs may first
appear to be irreconcilable, with ample motivation and creativity,
workable solutions may emerge.

> *Marguerite: When I was 51% sure I wanted us to go ahead and
> conceive, my partner Tay still had major reservations. Despite the
> skinny margin of my leaning towards having children, I took to
> heart my mother's wisdom not to wait for a mythical "better time."
> So I actively pursued working it out with Tay.*

> *Tay: Marguerite and I met as activists, and I cherished that shared
> connection. Our social change work felt core to me and I was
> afraid that if we had a child, all our energy would go to parenting,
> instead. So we "cut a deal," that within three years of having a
> child we'd do some important work out in the world together,
> whether volunteer or paid.*

A negotiation could work in either of these directions: toward having children or deciding not to. Following is an example in the
second direction.

Nina: Jack and I have used the decision-making processes in this guide for years, including for how many children to have.

Jack: I was happy with our family of two daughters and didn't want the responsibility of more children. Yet, right after Nina's beloved mother died, Nina was seized with yearning for more children and the chance to add a boy to our family. Her mother's death reminded her again of how much she had loved growing up in a large family.

Nina: Again and again, we returned to the Systematic Decision-Making Process [described in Chapter 4]. Finally, I realized that my leaning for more children was slight, flavored by ambivalence as well as yearning. Did I really want to go back to diapers? And even though I thought Jack's strong preference for a smaller family was colored by his own difficult childhood, collectively our leaning was clearly to stay with two children.

Jack: So we decided to not have more children.

Respect differences

Parenting is filled with losses and major challenges. Many couples deal with fertility and birthing losses: struggles to conceive, miscarriage, abortion, stillbirth, the disappointment of having a C-section instead of vaginal birth. Over the course of a lifetime, parents deal together with innumerable parenting-related losses or challenges, whether from the injuries, illnesses, and disabilities of their children, or simply from the loss of cherished hopes they had for them.

Often, each person in the couple processes deep emotions differently. One person may take a lot more time than the other, may be more expressive, or may interpret circumstances differently. As a couple, one of the hardest and most important things you can do for your relationship is to accept the different ways each of you grieve.

Our first child died in utero after a full nine months, just before Anne went into labor. Christopher's grief was a sudden rush, bringing up the loss of his mom who had died when he was 14. But within weeks of the stillbirth, he was eager to move on and to

> *absorb himself in work. In contrast, Anne's grief was sustained and physical; for months afterward, hard sobbing would overtake her without warning. The best thing we did for our relationship was to refrain from judging or blaming each other for our differences, and to each seek emotional support from other people (mostly, Christopher from other men and Anne from other women).*

While the challenge of a loss is more obvious, the differences in experiencing parenting joys also can be stressful for a couple. One parent may be delighted to attend every school play and recital, beaming with pride, while the other parent may find elementary school events too boring to tolerate.

Again, the key concept is to allow each person to parent in his or her own way, and to find new creative ways to meet the needs instead of getting snagged on judgments. For instance, in the above example, instead of feeling lonely and resentful, the parent who attends school plays could bring a loving friend as company, so they can beam together at the child. The parent who can't stand school recitals, instead of feeling judged as a bad parent, could find other ways 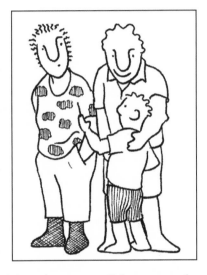 to show the child her interest and involvement. Of course, the child's needs are also a key part of the equation and need to be thoughtfully considered too.

Step out of limiting assumptions

We all make many assumptions, sometimes unconsciously, about what it means to be a good mother or a good father, and what it means to share the burdens and pleasures of parenting. If we're falling short of our own or our co-parent's expectations, what needs to change? Sometimes it's not our behavior but rather our assumptions.

> *Beth: When Angela and I chose to have a child via an anonymous donor, we both were happy with me carrying the child. Yet after our daughter, Nikki, was born, Angela struggled to bond with her. This continued for years and was terribly hard on our relationship. I judged Angela for not just "snapping out of it" and for not getting therapy about her own distant and judgmental mom, since I assumed her history was affecting her ability to parent.*

> *Angela: Finally, after Nikki was about 10 years old, a light bulb went off in my head. I was distant to my own mom, but very close to both my grandmothers. What if I "retired from being mom" and instead re-imagined myself as my daughter's grandmother?!*

> *Beth: This wacky idea finally has proved to be the biggest breakthrough of our parenting relationship. Previously, I was the permissive and empathetic parent and Angela was the uptight limit-setter. When Angela became "a grandmother" she could let go of nagging (do your chores, finish homework, get to bed) and focus instead on doing playful and connective*

> *activities with our daughter, as well as offering support to me.*

> *Angela: So that's what we did. Beth took on 98% of the daily parenting work (which she said actually felt easier because she could do it by her standards alone). I taught Nikki tennis and water-skiing and took her to concerts. If I wanted to nudge Nikki to do something, I had to suggest it to Beth, and she could choose to make the nudge or not. From this radical shift in roles, Nikki's and my relationship slowly and steadily improved, even during all her teenage years, when many moms and daughters are at loggerheads.*

There are many ways to structure good parenting relationships, so long as they work for all concerned. The important thing is to be aware of what's working and what's not working, and experiment with shifting the roles to better meet everyone's needs.

Exercise: Thinking out-of-the-box
List what roles each of you play as parents. Then each rate your level of satisfaction with these roles (from 1-10, with 1 as very low and 10 as very high). Each of you pick one role that had a low rating and brainstorm creative ways to change what isn't working for you. Discuss your brainstorm ideas and choose one or more new ways to play your role. Agree on a period of time to experiment; then evaluate the results.

So much more to say

Every couple faces different challenges and joys as parents. We're keenly aware that we address here only a few of our own, rather idiosyncratic challenges, which may be different from yours. Divorced families, blended families, same-sex couples, couples where a parent or child is disabled, where children are adopted... all these circumstances put different stresses on couple relationships. We also limited our comments here to how couples can get along better as they parent, leaving aside the enormous realm of parenting skills. We have already described in earlier chapters all the skills we have used to get along together as parents. Thus, this section is brief, even though the challenges of parenting are vast.

Parenting: key points

Learn from role models

> Talk about your parents and other couples' parenting
> What do you want to emulate?
> What do you want to do differently?

Negotiate big differences

> Use the Systematic Decision-making Process
> Think creatively
> Maximize meeting each person's needs

Respect differences

> Men and women often grieve differently
> Get support from your own gender
> Allow grief and joy to be expressed in your own ways
> Meet needs rather than judge each other

Step out of limiting assumptions

> Examine the roles each of you play as parents
> Consider out-of-the-box ways to meet needs

Aging together

At this writing, both of us are 57 years old. We know age is relative: Anne's mother, currently 92, views us as in the prime of life, but compared to our past selves, we feel bizarrely old. Every day we're confronted by our aging bodies, spirits, and identities, and by how these affect our relationship. Sometimes we're shocked and frightened by the extent of our wrinkles and gray hair, aches and pains, greater fatigue, and by how these are likely (if we're lucky!) to increase as we get older. Aging—oy!

We're also enormously grateful. How incredible to have had 32 (thus far) years of life experience together! We're deeply contented and comfortable: cooking a meal together… curling up together for a short nap almost every day after lunch… exclaiming together over the beauty of the sunset. These ordinary moments are joys we don't take for granted.

Much of the time, we find this peaceful ease delicious. Yet, at other times, our daily familiarity feels dull and confining. In fact, at this middle-aged juncture, our relationship feels filled with age-related contradictions and crosscurrents:

Committed to continuity, yet craving change. Many couples separate at this age, especially as children leave home. We're committed to staying together and building on the goodness of our lives, yet we're also hungry to experience adventure, growth, and change.

Thoroughly interdependent, yet desiring autonomy. Over the years, our possessions, finances, work, vacations, friendships, and memories have become increasingly shared. Even though we have always supported each other's growth, we're aware we may be limiting each other by our togetherness. We've been moving toward greater autonomy and time away from each other, and suspect it would growthful to do so even more.

Wonderfully secure, yet keenly vulnerable. More than ever, we're confident that we're together for life. However, along with this delicious security we feel keenly vulnerable. Disability or death might take either of us at any time. Friends our age and younger have already died.

If you and your partner have been together for decades, perhaps you relate to these cross-currents, and like us, are dealing with the twin challenges of being together a long time plus becoming middle-aged or old in this culture. Below are a few of the ways we're taking these on.

Renew your sexuality

Sooner or later, getting older confronts couples with the difference between past sexuality and current reality. Many feel uncomfortably disoriented by changed (and changing) bodies and declining response levels. It could be all-too-easy to take out feelings of loss on each other. Instead, it can be a good time to start new practices that remind each other you are allies, seeking to nurture your sexual connection as you become old. Here are a few practices that help us:

Get perspective by looking back at the present

Pretend that you and your partner are in your late 90's (or at least 10 years older than you are now). Exclaim with amazement as you "look back" at how young and able-bodied you are now.

> *Johnny, wow, how few wrinkles are on your face! Look at how easily you can get into bed!*

Mourn losses

Instead of trying to deny or minimize the sadness of pleasures lost, or leaping to "solve the problem," first join in and mourn the losses together with genuine and playful gusto.

> *Diane: Aargh, my orgasms are so elusive and mild compared to what they used to be!*
> *Brad: How sad and frustrating! No fair!*

Praise the new looks

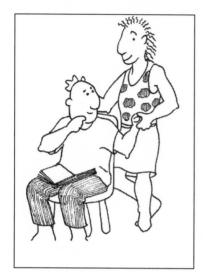

Most of us are terribly influenced by society's pervasive view of older people as unattractive, whether we intellectually believe it or not.

Whenever you can, offer genuine complimentary appreciations to counter your partner's negative self-image about looking old. Lay it on thick.

Sam, I love your beautiful white chest hair. Your bald head looks sexy to me!

Notice gains

Take time to notice what new pleasures of sensuality and connecting are opening up as arousal is far slower to build, without the "swept away" rush of hormones or early romance.

Now that my partner and I need to engage our imagination more to get aroused, we're having a great time reading erotica and sharing fantasies—something we didn't bother with before.

Acknowledge even tiny irritations

Over the first decade of our relationship we became proficient at processing misunderstandings and conflicts between us, using the skills described in the first part of this guide. Taking the time to quickly clear up annoyances was a fundamental part of our relationship. We called it the "Clean Windshield Commitment": if you wash the squished bugs and dirt off your car windshield daily, you have a lovely clear view of the world; if instead you let the bug crust stay on, it gets mighty hard to wash off. Eventually you think it's normal to look at the world through a dirty film. We're proud to have kept the windshield of our relationship clean and have avoided the painful relationship 'car wrecks' we've seen of some other couples.

Yet as we've entered our fourth decade together, and as Anne is in the thick of menopause, a new relationship challenge has arisen. We both feel barraged by micro-irritations, our name for annoyances that often seem too minor or too imbedded in the other's personality to bring up. They are tiny things that the other person may have no clue that we now find irritating. Maybe it's the way Christopher only likes his coffee in a carefully prepared way, or the way Anne pauses frequently in her sentences. Little things that were fine with us in earlier years now feel grating.

It can be tempting to keep micro-irritations to yourself:

> *Oh, it's just my stupid hormones making me so picky and thin-skinned. Such mundane things really shouldn't bother me. I don't want my partner to feel picked on or to walk on eggshells around me.*

Since it's your own fault for being bothered, is it better to keep these petty annoyances to yourself? Don't be fooled. Unprocessed irritations, especially tiny and repetitive ones, can become like a low-grade infection, constantly souring how you feel with your beloved. It's the hiding of irritations that give them power; if they are allowed or even welcomed, much of the negative charge dissolves. Taking the time to learn from little annoyances (using the many skills from this guide) will help keep the air between you clear.

A few suggestions:

> *Be sure to ask, "Is this a good time to process a micro-irritation?" Don't just leap in!*

> *Follow the processes suggested in the "Step out of Upsets, section" including taking turns, empathizing, and "The Glitch Process."*

> *You might develop a non-verbal signal (e.g. tugging your earlobe) to simply note that a micro-irritation has occurred. The other*

person nods to acknowledge the signal. Then you wait to discuss it when it's a good time and place. This is especially useful when at a restaurant with friends or other public place. Just the freedom to note it helps reduce the annoyance.

Even if processing micro-irritations is welcomed, the one receiving them can easily feel criticized. If irritations are frequent or one-sided, you might agree to save all processing for a pre-determined daily time when you both have good energy.

Be sure to balance the processing of irritations with exchanging lots of empathy and appreciations.

Some micro-irritations really are just fluff—a mood, a passing phase, something that evaporates once expressed. Other micro-irritations contain hidden nuggets of gold to offer the relationship. They point to needs that aren't getting fulfilled and changes you can easily make to increase each other's happiness. Enjoy your treasure hunt!

Question accommodation

In younger years, especially if you were juggling parenting or demanding careers, constant accommodation to each other's rhythms and needs may have seemed necessary.

As you age, these habitual accommodations may no longer be required or even tolerable. Especially for many menopausal women and empty-nesting mothers who spent a lifetime putting others' needs first, previously easy accommodations can feel to their nerves like the screech of fingernails on a blackboard. Have the two of you always gone to bed at the same time? Maybe it's time now to follow your own rhythms. When making daily decisions, has one of you usually gone along with the preferences of the other? Maybe that pattern no longer feels right. Relish the chance to look at old habits and decide anew.

Don't settle for boredom

If you've been together a long time and have many comfortable routines, it's easy for a layer of boredom to coat the relationship. Below are a few of the ways the two of us are looking to bring greater variety and enlivenment into our times together. Perhaps you would like to try them, too.

Small changes

Being inventive takes energy, something you may not always have. But as the documentary film "Happiness" revealed: even tiny differences in routines can add a surprising amount of zest to life. Think about small steps you can take: changing who sleeps on which side of the bed, who usually drives, what kind of music you listen to. Habits abound. Give them a jiggle.

Surprise dates

Make a "surprise date" at least once a month. One partner creates the plan; the other has no idea about what's to come. Each date, alternate who takes the lead. In addition to regularly scheduled surprise dates, if some good opportunity comes up either of you can propose a new surprise date at a specified time.

During the date, the recipient is encouraged to cheerfully go along with whatever is planned, whether or not it's his cup of tea. (They can have veto power if they find something truly objectionable.) Talking about what it's like to be in each role can be a valuable part of the date. What does it feel like to let go of control and be led? Is it relaxing? Scary? Fun? Like being a child? How about taking the lead? Does that feel powerful? Burdensome? Freeing? Experiencing different ways to follow or lead through having surprise dates can offer you a surprisingly rich amount to learn.

Playing with characters

Customary habits can feel glued to you like tight costumes you have forgotten how to remove. Sometimes our very personalities, familiar and beloved as they are, can feel tedious and tiresome. Yet to act differently from our norm can feel fake, a violation of being genuine.

Try shaking up rigid personas by taking on a character with different qualities than you usually manifest. (First make sure your partner is aware of your playful intentions!)

> ***Act out "disowned" or "shadow" parts.*** *For instance, Dani is almost always kind and gentle. She is enjoying playing with a new persona she is calling "Bitch," who has an attitude, and is blunt or nasty.*

> ***Act out desired qualities.*** *For instance, Charles wishes he would more often be light and expressive rather than tired and anxious. He once decided to attend the opening night of an arts conference as "Zim," a character who is bursting with friendliness, curiosity, brazenness, and zest. He had a much better time than usual!*

Play with improvisation exercises where you assume unfamiliar characters, roles, and situations. For instance, talk in pretend foreign accents.

Over time your characters might expand your repertoire of who you are, allow yourself to release uptightness, become more aware of shadow parts, develop more of your desired qualities, and have more fun.

Aging together: key points

Renew your sexuality

Get perspective by looking back at the present
Praise the new looks
Mourn losses
Notice gains

Acknowledge even tiny irritations

Make the "Clean Windshield" commitment
Agree to address micro-irritations
Use the Glitch Process and other tools
Develop a nonverbal signal
Balance frequent processing with appreciations

Question accommodation

Change old habits

Don't settle for boredom

Create small changes
Make surprise dates
Play with characters
- disowned qualities
- desired qualities
- improvisation games

Working Together

There are innumerable ways for couples to dedicate their combined energies towards "a greater purpose." Those who share a faith might fully participate together in their faith community; others who share political values might both campaign for candidates or attend rallies together. Some couples deliberately give to the world by building a loving home that serves as a welcoming haven. Many consider the raising of the next generation as the greatest purpose of their love. Whatever form it takes, there is beauty and meaning in knowing your love not only serves each other, but amplifies your ability to serve the wider community.

For us, working together as social entrepreneurs has served this purpose. Many couples are happy and fulfilled without combining their vocational lives. Yet for better or worse, jobs claim a major portion of most people's time. Sweethearts who can successfully join each other in paid work will likely spend more time together, and share more goals, challenges, and memories than couples that work separately.

Christopher: A life dream of mine was to work with a best friend. I gathered up my courage and propositioned Anne for us to work together.

Anne: At first I thought, "Are you kidding?? We're both so insecure about work. We'll just drag each other down!" But 23 years later, I can say that joining our work lives has helped us stay together. Far more than other common "glues" among couples (e.g. recreation), working together has been a reliably profound and pleasurable aspect our relationship.

Christopher: Because our work hasn't been mainly about making money, but about furthering causes to which we are fiercely dedicated, working together gives our love a deeper purpose. Together, we contribute something meaningful to the world – more effectively than either of us could do alone.

Many couples fear that the stress and power dynamics of working together could choke all nurturance out of their relationship. In our first years of working together, we certainly spent a lot of time processing difficulties using all the skills in this guide. Over time, we upset each other less and enjoyed ourselves more. We also developed some new tools and concepts specific to the challenges of working together.

Below are a few tools you might find useful in your work relationship, even if the work you do together is the unpaid labor of running a household or parenting.

Clarify decision-making roles

Many misunderstandings can be avoided by clarifying ahead of time who will be involved in making decisions and in what way. Whether you are part of a larger team or just working as a couple, gaining fluency with the roles below can be helpful.

Obviously, in situations where things work smoothly and organically you don't need to negotiate these roles. Unfortunately, even when you think you're clear, your partner (or others) may find the decision-making authority ambiguous or confused. That is where the model below can come in handy. While it was developed for decision-making in organizations, we've successfully used it for couples as illustrated by the examples here. (Read more in the "RAPID Decision-Making" article in the Resource section.)

Decision maker: Must be part of the decision.

For efficiency's sake, it's simplest to have just one of you make a decision. Yet for more complex or important decisions, you might want the wisdom that can come from both of you (or even a larger team) making the final decision together.

> *Janis: "William, I know you were going to decide the agenda for meeting with Ms. K, but I realized I need to be part of the meeting too and want to decide the agenda with you."*

Advisor: Does not make the decision, but must give feedback at one or more clearly named points in the decision-making process.

If you play the role of Advisor you need to be asked for input and give it early enough that you can suggest major changes in a timely way. (E.g., Ask your advisory partner for input on an article at least a week before a deadline, not the day before it is due for publication.) Make it clear whether your Advisor gives feedback once or multiple times, at which points in the process, and the date and time by which feedback must be given for it to be considered. The Advisor should clearly state which parts of her feedback she feels strongly about and which are more optional. The Decision-maker is not required to go along with the Advisor's recommendations, but if not, he may need to explain why.

> Zed: "Jim, I know I'm the decision-maker on this project, but could you advise me about how to make it more successful? I'd like to meet with you this week for the planning process and next week after I have a draft proposal done."

Input-giver: Is invited to give input by a specific date/time, but is not required to.

This difference between the Advisor (who is expected to respond to requests for feedback) versus an Input-giver (whose feedback is optional) is especially important in a larger team, when waiting for many responses can slow a project.

> Doris: "Liu, if you want to give me input on one or two additional people I should visit on this work trip to San Francisco, please give me their names by Tuesday at noon. If I don't hear from you I'll just settle the schedule myself."

Manager: Is responsible to move the decision to completion by a certain date.

Often the Manager of a decision is also Decision-maker. But this role can be delegated to someone else since simply moving a decision along can be a substantial organizing task in a big team.

Even as a couple, it can be helpful to state who will manage the decision.

> *Eleanor: "Mark, we need to decide together by Friday whether we're going to write that fundraising letter of inquiry. I'm flat out with meetings the next two days. Would you be willing to manage this decision so we don't miss the deadline?"*

Negotiate communication preferences

Sometimes even modest differences in communication styles can be challenging. Identifying key differences and making agreements about them— making it clear that no style is inherently "right" or "wrong"—can foster greater ease and harmony. Two examples:

Punch line versus story

Some people strongly prefer to hear the punch line or conclusion, without a lead-in story. Hearing the long version drives them wild with impatience to get back to work. Others enjoy the free expression of a longer story and the chance to vent feelings, as well as the pleasure of socializing, and find the punch line version unfriendly and constraining.

Punch line version:
> *Billy exclaims, "The printer is jammed. Can you help me?*

Story version:
> *Billy exclaims: "I got up so early this morning to work on that important grant proposal I've been sweating over all month. In fact, it is due by 5pm to-day. Everything was going really well, but when I tried printing the three charts at the end of the proposal the first two pages came out fine, but then something happened and the paper jammed. If*

I don't get this done on time, Jack will be really upset. Can you help?"

If you've talked about the differences, you can make agreements. For instance, anyone can say gently, "Punch line, please" and the others will understand the request. And those who enjoy longer versions can happily tell longer versions to each other. Or you can negotiate, "George, the punch line is that Melissa and I just had another big fight. I'm really upset and need to talk about what happened. Do you have some time right now?"

Interruptions

Some people prefer a work environment with lots of easy give-and-take. Why work together if you're not going to interact? Others really need quiet to keep their focus.

Those who tend to interrupt can learn to ask, "Could I ask you a quick question?" or "Would you have time today to help me think about something for five minutes?" instead of just launching in.

Those who prefer quiet focus can suggest regular times that work for interaction. "How about you save your questions, and every day after lunch we'll take 15 min. to go over them?" or "I could hold Thursday mornings as times when we talk together as we work. Would you like that?"

Offer feedback or advice skillfully

In theory, most of us value receiving personal feedback about our own performance or behavior, yet being offered advice unsolicited can sometimes feel like being scolded, patronized, or micro-managed. Even when we've asked for input, it's easy to get defensive. Here is a process that helps feedback sessions be more useful and friendly:

Check whether feedback is desired and when.

Shirley, would you like feedback on your facilitation of today's meeting? Yes? Would you prefer it now, or would some other time be better?

Clarify the process.

> *Would you first like to tell me your own assessment? Or would you like to hear my feedback first?*

Be specific and concise.

> *I'd like to tell you 3 things I liked that you did and 1-2 suggestions. How does that sound? (Offer more affirmation than constructive criticism.)*

Be ready to listen to feelings.

> *You sound upset. Would you like to vent for a minute about how frustrating it was, before I say any more?*

Help the recipient digest your feedback.

> *Was any of that useful to you? Do you have any questions about my suggestions?*

Nurture the relationship

Even if your work is inherently rewarding, the constant pressures and demands of work can erode the sweetness of a relationship (especially if it's on top of the demands of running a household and/or raising children). Also, if you're together nearly all the time, it may be hard to feel that lovely hunger for each other's company. To protect and regularly feed the pleasure of being together, you can develop rituals in three categories: boundaries, nourishment, and intimacies.

Boundaries on work time

Because work can expand to fill every moment given it, mutually agree upon some limits. For example:

- No work conversations before 9am or after 9pm.
- No work conversations during family time, dates or lovemaking.
- No venting about anything work-related that implicates the other person, unless you clearly forewarn your partner that the rant might trigger them, and then get their OK to proceed.
- Schedule time apart from each other (e.g., one day a week; one weekend a season).

Nourishment

If you work at home or have control over your work environment, take advantage of it. Use the freedom to develop rituals that nourish your relationship. These nourishing rituals can include and benefit other staff as well. For example:

- Cook and eat special lunches together.
Put on favorite soothing or energizing music when working.
Put on a favorite dance song and take a dance break.

Intimacies

So long as you are respectful of others around you, you don't need to act like "normal" co-workers do. You can harness the healing power of your closeness to have a better workday. For example, especially if you work at home, you can:

- Briefly nap or meditate together after lunch.
- Have difficult work conversations lying in each other's arms.
- When no one is around, surprise your partner with a kiss.

Introduce new initiatives carefully

Couples that work together, especially in their own business or as entrepreneurs, can easily become polarized when one person tends to be visionary and the other pragmatic. In that painful dance, the Visionary feels her creativity is squashed because the Pragmatist responds with anxiety when any new idea is proposed. "Why are you already scowling? I've barely let the words out of my mouth!" The Pragmatist resents being cast as the bad guy, when he is just trying to be realistic and keep the team from getting overwhelmed. "How can you suggest a big new project now? You know we have no money to hire more staff!"

Here is a process for considering new ideas that can cut through this polarity and help both sides relax. Even when couples (or groups) are not polarizing, they may find this process helpful.

Step 1: Contract for time to raise a new possibility

Rather than blurting out his new ideas and expecting excited response, the Visionary carefully helps the Pragmatist be ready to hear his thoughts. "I've got a new idea I'd like to explore. It's not a proposal. I don't know if I'd want us to do it. But I want some receptive space to explore it together. Is now a good time?"

Step 2: Acknowledge context and understand intentions

First, the Visionary briefly acknowledges any prior relevant context or agreements. ("I know we've said we don't want to supervise more workers.") Then, he encourages the Pragmatist to put her anxiety aside, to empathize with his visionary impulse and the intentions behind it, to ask open-ended questions to better understand the intentions, and to make whatever positive comments she genuinely can. No negative comments or concerns are expressed at this stage.

Step 3: Discuss concerns

Now the Pragmatist and Visionary can both name concerns about the idea and make sure they understand each others' interests. Often misunderstandings are revealed in the discussion. ("Oh, I thought you meant...!") Then do an initial brainstorm of ways to address those concerns.

If both parties then agree that the idea seems worth seriously considering, go on to Step 4. If not, hopefully you've at least had a constructive and stimulating conversation instead of a fight.

Step 4: Flesh out a proposal

If the idea is worth seriously considering, take time to spell it out in enough detail so that it can be more fully evaluated. This might be a process over days or weeks. Do whatever research is needed in order to propose in writing the goals, budget, and work plan.

Step 5: Address concerns

Again, both the Visionary and Pragmatist look at the proposal and discuss together how to address concerns. Ideally, get input from others.

Step 6: Decide

Make a decision whether or not to move the initiative into implementation. Remember, at any stage, the idea can be acknowledged for its potential value and then shelved or released.

This process is useful not only in working together, but for any of the innumerable large work commitments couples take on together: renovating a home, having another child, living a year abroad... It can be useful instead of or in addition to the Systematic Decision-Making Process (earlier in this guide) whenever a decision being considered would generate a good deal of work for both parties.

Build on strengths and address limitations

In any good work team, members usually get to know each other's strengths and weaknesses and divide the work accordingly. But when couples work together, divisions of labor can become touchy. The less competent partner (in a given area) may feel embarrassed, abandoned, or judged; the more competent partner (in a given area) may feel burdened, frustrated, and resentful. These differences may get further aggravated through gender roles and patterns, as well as with tensions you experience outside the workplace.

It can help to explore this with gentle awareness. See if you can come to agreement about each other's different strengths and limitations. Make a conscious decision together about when you'll build on existing strengths, and when and how to address limitations.

Jill has a history of writing blocks and still freezes on first drafts. Yet she is a competent editor once a draft is written. Jill happily agreed to have her partner Samantha write all the first drafts, and she is gaining writing confidence by being the editor.

Billy is "good at guy things" such as fixing office equipment, dealing with the computer, and managing the project finances. So without discussion, he slipped into those roles. Once they discussed it, he and his partner Sarah agreed that she'd take the finances off his shoulder: she could feel more empowered and he become less burdened. Billy still is the main point person for the technology.

Both Elsa and Robert avoid making the desperately needed sales calls, so finally they hired a sales manager, Melissa, who delights in that work.

The book *Move to Greatness* describes four types of leadership energy needed for effective projects and organizations: (1) organizer, (2) visionary, (3) driver, and (4) collaborator. Ideally, everyone develops all four competencies, but of course each person has natural strengths and weaknesses.

We find this model easier to communicate to a team than the better-known and also useful Myers-Briggs or Enneagram personality models. As a couple in leadership, attending to these four qualities has helped us appreciate our individual qualities and to bring in other team members to build a full complement of different strengths.

Christopher's strong visionary energy is fortunately complemented by Anne's strong organizer energy. Christopher has great driver energy, and Anne is learning from him how to move a project forward. They both have strong collaborator energy with people they enjoy, but Christopher wants to become a better collaborator in situations where there is a less easy stylistic match with teammates.

Face the complications of co-leading as a couple

Sometimes being part of a couple that is leading an organization or a team can make things easier for you. When one of you wakes up at 3am with an anxiety attack, the other is already fully briefed for the ad hoc emergency strategy session! You can provide each other with a level of support, both emotional and practical, that would be impossible if you didn't both know each other and the work so well.

However, there can be complications that bite you. These are especially nasty if you're caught unaware, so here are a few of touchy issues to keep an eye out for:

Parental projection: Especially if you are a man and a woman running the show, your staff, clients, board members, and other stakeholders may see you as Mom and Dad. And this is especially difficult if they have had problematic relationships with either or both parents.

Assumptions about communication: Your team members may assume that if they have spoken to one of you, the other will be told about it, which may not necessarily be the case.

Complaints or playing one off the other: If team members find one of you more accommodating or easier to negotiate with, they may avoid the other or complain about him to you, rather than going directly to him to work things out.

When you catch dynamics like any of the above, take them seriously. Discuss them first with each other and then with your team. Know it may take many conversations to shift these patterns.

Working together: key points

Clarify decision-making roles

Decision-maker
Advisor
Input-giver
Manager

- from Jon Huggett and Caitrin Moran, RAPID Decision-Making

Negotiate communication preferences

Talk about differences of style. For example:
- prefer punch line versus prefer full story
- prefer boundary versus prefer easy exchange

Offer feedback or advice skillfully

Check if and when feedback is desired
Clarify the process
Be specific and concise
Offer more affirmation than criticism
Be ready to listen to feelings
Help the recipient digest your feedback

Nurture the relationship

Make boundaries on work time
Add nourishment to your work day
Be energized by intimacies

Introduce new initiatives carefully

1. Contract for time to raise a new possibility
2. Acknowledge the context and understand intentions
3. Discuss concerns
4. Flesh out a proposal
5. Address concerns
6. Decide whether to implement the new initiative

Build on strengths and address limitations

Balance the four types of leadership energy:
Visionary
Organizer
Driver
Collaborator

- from Ginny Whitelaw and Betsy Wetzig, Move To Greatness

Face the complications of co-leading

Parental projections
Assumptions about communication
Playing one off the other

Closing

We relied heavily on the tools in this book to get along with each other through this big writing project. Many times the stress of writing together (on top of other demands) triggered old patterns and irritations—just so we don't get too smug! We needed every skill: taking turns... interrupting patterns... exchanging empathy and appreciation... and we must have used "the glitch process" dozens of times.

The tools came alive for us. We were not only re-inspired by their usefulness, but also recognized freshly where we needed to add more nuances to the older text. We also felt humbled by the places where we have yet to hone our own mastery.

Despite these glitches, our pleasure at co-creation far outweighed the annoyances. What could be more satisfying than working shoulder-to-shoulder with someone you love, creating a gift of value to others?

Reflect for connection

And so, our learning continues, and we trust the same is true for you. At the beginning of the book we described four skill-learning stages that help us relax into the confusion and awkwardness of trying new skills. In closing we'd like to offer another generically useful tool we created to support our learning: a reflection process. Might you like to try it now, to reflect on your experience reading this guide?

Current education theory suggests that learning comes from a cycle of experience and reflection. An optimal ratio of reflection to experience is at least two to one. Yet many of us live such pressured lives that we give little time to reflect on more than even a small fraction of the many experiences in our typical day.

Taking time to reflect daily on your life, even briefly, can help you to release tensions (before they accumulate in your internal organs and do damage), to learn from your life experience, and to be more in touch with yourself and with your partner.

We developed this model below to do satisfying reflection together in just 15-20 minutes. Although it is simple it has been so valuable to us that we use it nearly every day. Take turns with each question.

Reflection process

Highlights:
What are three things you enjoyed?

Accomplishments:
What are two things you are proud of?

Challenge:
Name one thing that was hard for you.
What's a lesson you take from it?

Appreciation:
Name something you're grateful for in your life or in your relationship.

We use this simple reflection format all the time to savor our experience and to highlight learning: when we're alone writing in our journals, when we're traveling apart from each other and have just a few minutes on the phone together in which to get connected, at birthday dinners to reflect on the past year, and nightly, when one of us turns to the other before sleep and whispers: "Hey, what are three highlights of your day?"

Be in touch

We've surprised ourselves with how much pleasure we got from writing down the tools in this guide and are excited to share them with you. Please adapt them to be more useful to you, and share the guide or any portion of it with your friends and loved ones.

We'd love to hear from you about your experience in using any of the tools. We offer phone or in-person consultations, workshops, and Playback Theatre performances on relationship themes (using improvisational theatre for empathy and appreciation of true stories people share from their lives).

With gratitude for all those who make love a skillful practice,

Anne and Christopher
Anne@TrueStoryTheater.org
Still on the trapeze, 2013

Resources for chapters 1-5

Communication and personal growth skills

Cameron-Bandler, Leslie. (1985) *Solutions: Practical and Effective Antidotes for Sexual and Relationship Problems.* San Rafael, CA: Future-Pace, Inc.. Detailed description of approaches from neuro-linguistic programming applied to couples therapy.

Carson, Richard D. (2003) *Taming Your Gremlin.* New York: Quill. An amusing and profound book on how to love yourself.

Gordon, Thomas. (2001) *Leader Effectiveness Training.* New York, Perigee Trade. An invaluable set of skills for listening, assertiveness and problem-solving, applicable to everyone.

Hendrix, Harville. (2007) *Getting the Love You Want.* New York: Harper and Row. A marvelously wise guide to working through the obstacles to a partnership that works. Contains many valuable exercises.

Madson, Patricia Ryan. (2010) *Improv Wisdom: Don't Prepare, Just Show Up.* New York: Random House. A clear, concise book of key principles of improvisations, useful to everyday life.

Re-evaluation co-counseling: A world-wide network providing peer counseling. One 16-week class provides a lifetime of essential emotional literacy. Don't be scared off by the organizational rigidity and weird jargon. Take what's useful and leave behind the rest. See: www.RC.org

Rosenberg, Marshall. (2003) *A Model for Nonviolent Communication.* Philadelphia: New Society Publishers. A short exercise book to help develop simple but potent communication skills for resolving conflict. Nonviolent communications workshops are offered online and world-wide. See: www.CNVC.org

Sexuality

Brauer, Alan P. and Brauer, Donna J. (April 2001). *ESO: How You and Your Lover Can Give Each Other Hours of Extended Sexual Orgasm.* In addition to the orgasm tips, this book includes great exercises for releasing resentments and increasing communication.

Daedone, Nicole. (May 2012) *Slow Sex.* Grand Central Life & Style. Describes a surprisingly powerful 15-minute practice of "orgasmic meditation" to enhance sexual ease and connection.

Deida, David. (March 2006). *The Way of the Superior Man: A Spiritual Guide to Mastering the Challenges of Women, Work, and Sexual Desire.* Controversial and thought-provoking.

Easton, Dossie and Hardy, Janet W. (March 2009). *The Ethical Slut: A Practical Guide to Polyamory, Open Relationships & Other Adventures.* A landmark book about exploring conscious, respectful, non-monogamous relationships.

Gass, Robert and Ansara, Judith. Wise and skillful trainers whose retreat for long-time couples made a difference in our relationship. See: http://sacredunion.com/couples/deepening-in-love/

Love, Patricia Love and Robinson, Jo. (June 2012). *Hot Monogamy: Essential Steps to More Passionate, Intimate Lovemaking.* A thorough, practical, fun guide for long-term relationships, whether monogamous or not.

Singer, Katie (April 2004). *The Garden of Fertility: A Guide to Charting Your Fertility Signals to Prevent or Achieve Pregnancy—Naturally...* Not to be confused with "the rhythm method," this fully reliable method also increases self-knowledge and communication.

Taylor, Patrica. (November 2001). *Expanded Orgasm: Soar to Ecstasy at Your Lover's Every Touch.* Naperville, Illinois: Sourcebooks

Casablanca. Despite the hokey title, a mind-opening book about being fully present rather than goal-oriented during sex.

Money

The Bolder Giving Workbook: includes a simple one-page template for a giving plan and references to more sophisticated giving plan advice. Free download available at www.BolderGiving.org

Collins, Victoria. (1997). *Couples and Money*: Encino, CA: Gabriel Publications. A very readable guide with simple tools to help couples manage their finances and their relationship.

Leondar-Wright, Betsy. (2005). *Class Matters: Cross-class Alliance-Building for Middle Class Activists*. New Society Publishers. Full of stories, photos, cartoons, and tips on how work well with people of different class backgrounds.

Mellan, Olivia and Christie, Sherry. (2013). *Money Harmony: A Road Map for Individuals and Couples*. Money Harmony Books. Smart models and exercises to help couples navigate differences.

More than Money Journal: 43 issues of the journal available for free download. Full of stories and practical wisdom on how to put our money and values together. Look especially at the issues on Money and Couples (#5), Cross-Class Relationships (#17), and Money and Relationships (#40). See: MoreThanMoney.org.

Robin, Vicki. (2008). *Your Money or Your Life*. Penguin Books. An out-of-the-box roadmap of how to retire from money-making sooner rather than later, simplify your life, and focus on realizing your greatest gifts.

Parenting together

Markova, Dawna with Powell, Annie. (1996). *How Your Child is Smart: A Life-Changing Approach to Learning*. Conari Press. A sophisticated model explaining visual, kinesthetic and auditory learning styles, useful for couples as well as parents.

RC family work: Browse the literature at www.rationalisland.com (search for "family" or "parenting").

Working together

Huggett, Jon and Moran, Caitrin. (2008) Bridgespan Group article "RAPID Decision-Making: What it is, why we like it, and how to get the most out of it." A simple but powerful model of different key roles for decision-making. It's downloadable for free on the Social Enterprise Alliance Knowledge Center website.

Hanson, Birgit Zacher and Hanson, Tom (August 2010). *Who Will Do What by When?* Power Publications. A simple guide to a critical practical need.

Hawley, Miriam (Author), with McIntyre, Jeffrey (Aug 21, 2012). *You & Your Partner, Inc.: Entrepreneurial Couples Succeeding in Business, Life and Love.* Enlignment Inc. Interviews and insights from many couples who have worked together.

Stewart-Gross, Becky L. and Gross, Michael J. (July 2007). *Sleeping with Your Business Partner: A Communication Toolkit for Couples in Business Together.* Capital books. Offers many tips on improving communication and teamwork.

Whitelaw, Ginny and Wetzig, Betsy (Dec 4, 2007). *Move to Greatness: Focusing the Four Essential Energies of a Whole and Balanced Leader.* Nicholas Brealey. Offers images and movement exercises to strengthen leadership energies in an interesting model.

Chapter 6

Out-of-the-box loving

Chapter 6: Out-of-the-box loving (by Alyssa Lynes)

Why I am a part of this book

This book has traveled with me around the world the last few years, acting as a reference, a support, a guide, always offering me relief that I am not alone in my experience loving. I have shared it with lovers and friends and also turned to it alone in moments when I needed some perspective. I am honored to add my points of view and share some of my own experiences. My wish for you, the reader, is to both inspire a sense of possibility and offer some additional resources.

I first read "Getting Along" while in a monogamous relationship. I reread it while in an open relationship that we committed to stay in for one year. Within that year I read it again and again, sometimes alone and other times with my partner. We discussed what chapter might support us during many different growing moments. We looked at it when we engaged intimately with others, together and separately. We traveled, worked together and managed finances. We lived in a small RV seeing each other almost exclusively. We also connected long distance from different countries. Ultimately, we graciously transitioned into becoming loving friends (uncoupling).

Since then, I have read "Getting Along" while being single, when dating one person at a time, and as I came out more fully to identify as polyamorous. I now teach somatic workshops and coach people around intentional relationships. I see many possibilities for myself and others in designing the relationships that best nourish us.

When I look back, I can see a number of key moments when a book like this could have influenced my choices. I imagine I would have had less anxiety and more graceful approaches to life-long loving.

Times I could have used this book... :

- As I told my college boyfriend that I cheated on him.
- As I discussed agreements for my solo trip to Latin America with a monogamous partner.
- As I was deciding whether to propose to marry my partner of 6 years and when I broke it off.
- As I explored bilingual and bicultural relationships in my own country and in other countries.
- As I navigated long distance relationships with phone & video dating and sex.
- As I facilitated festivals and workshops on intimacy and communication.
- As I came out to my parents as polyamorous.

Christopher and Anne have generously demonstrated how they grew together within a committed relationship that has shifted over time to include many elements beyond love and romance such as: a shared home, a child, working together, aging together and finances. While I am open to having many of these things all within one relationship, I am actively interested in exploring filling the different potential special roles in my life with multiple people. These roles may include: a creativity project partner, a romantic living-together partner, a long-distance phone call lover, an occasional visiting lover, a collaborative parent, a biological father to our child. They may each satisfy different kinds of connection and intimacy. I may collaborate artistically with one and turn to another for emotional support or sexual expression. I may come home to yet another person with whom I share the gift of raising children.

In talking with Christopher and Anne about the book, we realized that I could contribute perspectives that broaden the conversation about getting along and skills for life-long loving. I appreciate that the book now includes the four sections I have written on long-distance relationships, uncoupling, polyamory, and finding your partner. In each of these chapters, I offer guidance on how you can have successful, loving relationships that are out-of-the-box of what is often considered possible.

I'd love to hear about your experiences and receive your feedback. Please feel free to reach out to me if I can support you in any way.

alyssalynescoaching@gmail.com
https://alyssalynes.com

Long distance relationships

Strengthening your connection with your partner when in different places can add to the beauty of the relationship and support each of you individually. One or both of you might be in a new environment and the consistency of support and of loving or sexy interactions will nourish and enable you to bring yourselves more fully to those around you.

Many couples worry if they plan to be apart for a time. While in different places, people often put their attention on longing to be together and on the frustration of being out of physical contact with their love. Instead of spending energy on what is not possible you may appreciate the unique creative ways you can learn to connect with loved ones from a distance.

This section focuses on how we can better enjoy the experience of being in connection while in different locations and provides tools to support intimacy from afar. You will find tips on how to use the framework of the Five Love Languages to be more present and creative in your long-distance loving. You will read about the importance of recognizing time agreements and discover suggestions for fun date night possibilities.

For the sake of clarity, this chapter is written using the partnership model of two people. These tips can also be applied to polyamorous partnerships or constellations.

Love Languages for long distance connecting

How do you and your partner experience love? What would make each of you feel thought of and cared for while being apart? Gary Chapman first wrote about the Five Love Languages in 1995, and since then it has been a useful framework that many people turn to in order to express how they can best receive and experience love. While there are many helpful approaches to refer to, we will use the Five Love Language model to explore how to love long distance.

1. Words of affirmation long distance

Letters, emails, texts, and phone conversations are filled with words. People who thrive on receiving love in the form of encouraging words may feel at ease with long distance communication. Others may want to put more effort into exploring how words can support them to feel connected and loving from a distance. You may find yourself increasing words of affirmation during these times apart to fill in for a love language (such as touch) that is not available in this context.

Get out of your comfort zone. Sometimes your sense of identity is linked to how words are used. If using words to express your connection is unfamiliar or awkward for you, be compassionate with yourself. You might consider it as a meaningful game to try out verbalizing what you are feeling toward your partner. Let them know how you feel and try exploring words together. You might find a different part of yourself can be expressed.

Be specific. While you might not see each other and can't touch each other, details can especially support people to get on the same page. When your partner shares a specific reason or moment they noticed and appreciated you may be more able to receive it, believe it, and take it in.

A few examples with details:

"I so appreciate how you called me right at the time you said you would! It's really great to hear your voice."

"I love how you tell me all the spices you are cooking with. It gives me such a sensory experience while we are talking."

"You made the kids brownies on their snow day this week! What a loving dad you are!"

"Thanks for helping my Grandma move last weekend. I really appreciate you helping the family while I'm away!

"I feel totally at home with you as we are talking. Just being with you on the phone is helping me relax after a stressful day. Thanks for making yourself available to chat last minute."

2. Acts of service long distance

People who receive love through acts of service feel valued and cared for when the giver does so out of choice and not obligation. From a distance an act of service may come in the form of skill sharing, recommendations or referrals. Seeing these recommendations and referrals as a language of love supports connection.

Share skills

Some examples of skill sharing that can be explained via words or video are listening when someone needs emotional support, giving computer advice and providing financial planning ideas.

I needed to put my bike in the back of my small car. I called my partner who directed me over the phone to remove the tire. I felt cared for, could drive home with my bike, and learned a new skill.

Make recommendations:

"Why don't you watch this Facebook link of a short dance video?"

"Check out this instructional video on how to resolve your computer issue."

"I think you'll like this Audible book. Here's the link to download it."

Offer referrals

Support the well-being of your partner by connecting them to people who can provide local services.

I suggest you go to this chiropractor who I saw last time I was in New York.
I have a great friend in Berlin you should meet for coffee. I think it's fun to meet friends of friends when traveling alone. Have a great adventure!

3. Receiving gifts long distance

Some people thrive on the thoughtfulness and effort behind gifts. Receiving a letter in the post may seem even more special now that it is often a novelty. Some material gifts may include sweet post-cards, a delivery of massage oil directly from the online store, or a copy of this book.

4. Physical touch long distance

For the person whose primary love language is touch, it's especially important to approach a long distance relationship with creativity and to stay open to new possibilities. It may be a process to let go of feeling shy or awkward in order to more deeply connect to people on phone dates. Here are a few ways to bring touch into the long distance experience:

Touch yourself

Link the sensation of touch to being with your partner. This kinesthetic experience can help you receive the warmth they are sending you through your skin. This self touch can include all the varied energies that touch can explore: loving, sensual, spiritual, playful, sexual...

Simply touch yourself while connecting with your partner.

> *I put a calm hand on my face or give myself a little caress while feeling the loving energy of my sweetheart talking to me on the phone.*

Use massage. Roll on a massage ball or gently squeeze a sore muscle.

> *When my husband is away on business, I love giving myself a foot massage when we talk. It is something he does for me at home so it feels extra sweet to do together while we are physically apart.*

Use video

Include your partner in your touch experience by being seen on video.

> *I felt awkward and nervous at first but now I like using video. When my partner can see me, I have more choice as to how much I use words and how much I express with my body.*

Use words to connect and get creative
You can choose to tell your partner you are touching yourself or not. You may tell them via the phone or by text.

Choose who does what to whom
You can touch yourself while with your partner on the phone and share verbally about what you are doing. Your partner can do the same, telling you what she is doing with her body. You can word it as though your touch to yourself is representing what your sweetie would be doing to you or what you want to do to her. You also may have fun saying what you want her to do to her own body.

You can get creative playing with these options of touching. You may bring in a prop or toy to show how you would interact with your partner. It might be full of images and poetic or raunchy and kinky. One person may be the dominant one and say all the words or you may go back and forth. You can have different sessions of leading and following.

Choose when the fantasy happens
Get creative with your tenses and see what feels most connective and exciting in the moment.

Use words to describe what you wish you were doing right now:

- I would love to be running my fingers slowly down your back.
- I am kissing your right earlobe and whispering to you.

Use words to describe a memory of a sensual or sexual time you actually shared in physical reality.

- Remember when I laughed....
- I loved that time when you bounced up and down on the mattress and wrestled me to the floor.

Use words to create a scene that you want to enact in the future.

- When I pick you up at the airport I'm going to squeeze you so hard.
- When you get home to me, I will run you a bubble bath and light candles.

Use words to create a fantasy scene that may never be enactable.

- We are lying in a tent in a magical forest. It's pouring outside. I am kissing your feet and removing your high heels. OMG! There's a loud monstrous sound coming from the swamp! Did you bring your superpowers?

5. Quality time long distance

For some people, receiving undivided attention from their partner says "I love you" like nothing else. This can be spending uninterrupted time together, talking or doing an activity. When we clarify our wishes around quality time and make agreements, we can celebrate and enjoy our interactions more fully. It may take a little extra communication to get on the same page.

Ask yourself the following questions:
What are my current expectations of my partner with regard to how we share time?

- Frequency of planned quality time or date nights
- Response time to messages
- Unplanned communications

Are we on the same page about our expectations or is there something to get clearer on so we can enjoy both the planned time together and the extra spontaneous communications?

Agree on time commitments

Here's an example of a clear time arrangement.

> *Josh can count on having date night via video chat for 3 hours with Alex on Sunday night and a 30 minute phone chat on Tuesday. He looks forward to those times with excitement. Alex and Josh have said they will send each other one text a day to share an important moment or a silly image or photo. They understand that there is no commitment to respond right away to these texts. They enjoy getting a text back by the end of the day when possible. If they want a response by a set time or some correspondence beyond these agreements they can ask for it. All extra texts, emails, or calls are unexpected and sweet surprises.*

Agree on response time to messages

> *At one point, I was dating three people long distance. Each one was set up differently, and as long as I adjusted my expectations appropriately I could enjoy all of them. Jorge, I came to recognize, would respond to a text usually within 36 hours whereas Doug, within 5 minutes and Jasper by the end of the day.*
>
> *One time I wrote Jorge a vulnerable text about having had an important conversation with a metamor (another lover of his). After 12 hours of no response I felt annoyed and I noticed that I was beginning to judge him as inconsiderate. In reality, I did not know what his day looked like and based on his norm of not responding prior to 36 hours, this was probably not a ruthless response. He was doing nothing out of the ordinary. The change was that I felt vulnerable when I wrote that text and wished for a faster reply. He didn't know this shift and so I needed to be more clear and ask directly for a response sooner.*
>
> *I wrote Jorge:*
>
> > *"Wishing for a little response from u to feel complete in this step of communication. Can you let me know u received this? ♥♥✈ I'm off."*
>
> *By the time I landed from my flight, he had written back:*

"I'm so glad you all had such a kickass, clarifying, and compassionate chat. That makes me so happy, and I'm so glad it went well."

I was relieved and warmed by his response. More importantly, I could see how I wished to avoid judging him. I learned that I needed to communicate clear requests when I wanted a response by a specific time or for a timing that was out of our established norm.

Acknowledge a shift in timing

Imagine you are in a room together.
Your lover seductively says: *I want to kiss you in the sunshine.*
You promptly respond: *'TTYL'* or *'gotta run'* and leave the room.
Sounds a bit jarring, right?

This is how it might feel via text also. When a rate of communication has been established and you can no longer continue with this rate of attention, let your partner know that you have to make a shift and whenever possible leave a moment for closure.

Communicate what they can expect next from you

Write them that you have to go back to work or focus on something else. This way it is clear that the reason you are pausing your conversation is because you need to focus on something else. This may decrease the chance of them creating a story about why you stopped chatting with them. They know you are occupied and they can't expect fast responses to further texts.

Give a moment for closing remarks

They may want to send a closing text before you put the phone on airplane mode and disappear. If you give a warning that you have to go in a few minutes you can collaborate on the closure of the conversation.

> *One lover and I wrote many spontaneous texts a day. Based on our availability in that moment we would establish a rate of communication. Sometimes one of us sent out a flirty comment and the other would respond 3 hours later after our work was through. Sometimes we got into chatting, sexting or flirting back and forth in that moment as though in a live conversation.*

> *I found that if the rate of responses shifted drastically without warning or acknowledgement, my perception of the fun conversation could abruptly change so that I felt unsettled or annoyed. Now, when we are no longer available to continue at the same rate, we write something like this:*

> *"This was so fun. Thanks. I can spend 2 more minutes with you and then I have to go back to work. Want to continue at 10:00pm and put me to bed?"*

Long distance date nights

1. Schedule the date ahead of time. Commit to be together. Know the start time and if you have a set end time or not. Decide if you are setting aside other distractions during your date. By making these agreements ahead you can anticipate having each other's attention. You can also look forward to your date and prepare for it as you might with an in-person date.

2. Create a plan. There are many fun things to do together. It can be great to brainstorm things you would like to do and then know which one is coming. Here are a few ideas to try:

- Cook the same meal separately, but eat together on the call.
- Watch a movie at the same time in your separate beds.
- Go out to a cafe together via video chat.
- Take a walk and show each other your favorite park nearby.
- Take a bubble bath together via phone.
- Turn off the lights and then say goodnight. Cuddle up to two separate pillows. Then bookend the sleeping together

date by calling each other when you wake up in the morning, all sleepy sounding.

3. Prepare your space and energy. How can you get in the mood for the upcoming date? Maybe you want to take a shower as a way to release stress from the day, put all the laundry and computer work to the side, put on sexy clothes, prepare your space with candles, etc.. Do whatever it is that prepares you to be fully present with just that person on the call.

4. Enjoy the date.

5. Close the date with celebration and clarity. At the end of an in-person date a conclusive moment usually happens. This might be a hug or kiss. Here you could consider using some words of affirmation instead. You might say something you appreciate about your date or something you are grateful for. You could also clarify when you'll next connect. Ideally you leave the date feeling loved up and clear about when you'll meet next.

> *I loved that moment when you told me to let my hair down and imagine you nuzzling my neck. I can't wait until our next date on Wednesday. The cafe I'm taking you to is so sweet.*

Essentially, be bold. Discover something new about yourself, and aim to strengthen the relationship despite or even because of this distance. Even though we may see some of these tools as new or edgy for us, by trying them out we get to develop together differently. Talking through love languages and exploring how to demonstrate those from a distance can set the stage for further growth and connection. Regardless of the medium you use to communicate, find ways to be present in the moment to appreciate the quality of your time together. Seek new possibilities for creative expression and discover a variety of ways to love and support each other.

Long distance relationships: key points

Explore the "five love languages" long distance

Words of affirmation, acts of service,
  receiving gifts, physical touch, quality time

Explore physical touch while on the phone

Touch yourself, sensually or sexually
Use video
Use words creatively: fantasies, memories, future touch
Play with who directs the touching

Plan for quality time by phone

Make clear agreements: frequency of dates, response
  time to messages, unplanned communications
Acknowledge shifts of expectation
Create a moment of closure

Create long distance date nights

1. Schedule the date ahead of time
2. Create a plan
3. Prepare your space and energy
4. Enjoy the date
5. Close the date with celebration and clarity

Uncoupling: ending a partnership

You might ask why there's an uncoupling chapter in a book on life-long love? Uncoupling can be seen as a very important moment in which we have an opportunity to demonstrate being loving and respectful at a vulnerable time. A thoughtful, positive experience of separating can help you make a clean break, set the foundation for a new version of relationship with that person, and/or send you each on your individual paths with clarity. It will help deepen the communication skills you take into any future loving relationships.

Uncoupling can occur in any kind of relationship. If there are more than two people involved, as in a polyamorous relationship, this chapter can be creatively adapted to support everyone affected. For the sake of clarity, the wording in this chapter will focus on two people.

Included in this chapter is a 'moving on' story of Alyssa's, some suggestions for closing, letting go, and moving forward, alone or with help from others. You can find tips to create a ritual and find support. Regardless of what you do, you want to look back at this process of uncoupling and know you gave it your all.

Time to move on: Alyssa's story

We had been living together for five years and we were engaged. I knew that a lot of my interests were not shared with him. Non-violent communication led me to realize that I could have many of my needs met outside the relationship. I began traveling to more dance events and went camping with my best friend instead of with my partner. I sent sweet emails home and had connective phone calls from a distance with him when I was away and we still kept increasing our time apart. He was considering mortgages on a home, prioritizing his needs for stability and comfort, while I, meanwhile, was excited to travel internationally again. I began to consider uncoupling.

To find more clarity I asked friends for their opinions. A few key questions they asked me stayed with me.

Do you feel like he is really your soulmate?

Are you willing to be his partner for life?

Are your visions for life partnership aligned?

Do you remember that time when it was so difficult to be with him?

While these conversations were hard and I often felt defensive at first, it was helpful to have perspective from my community and hear their memories of what I had experienced.

After becoming engaged, we went to a few premarital sessions with a Unitarian Universalist minister. The minister asked us to consider the possibility that neither of us would ever change. Given that all our differences would remain throughout our lives, did we still want to be married to each other?

Ultimately, I ended the relationship and moved out. While I felt sad and went through a mourning process, I knew I had come to clarity and could communicate what I understood to him in a respectful way. I told him that I believed that we had different priorities, needs and life visions. This felt like a compassionate way to acknowledge that we were no longer moving in the same direction and we could look at each other as dignified individuals on separate paths. I could express a lot of gratitude while acknowledging we were no longer a fit. This courageous conversation lead us to uncouple while we had only an apartment, some belongings and a shared bank account to negotiate. I feel grateful for having my friends and NVC as resources that helped me recognize this prior to getting married.

Safety first

Your safety comes first. It's important to acknowledge that getting out of an abusive relationship may take different considerations that are not expanded upon here. First and foremost, plan for your own safety and find the support to help you. Regardless of the situation you are leaving, be gentle with yourself and ask for support from others as you make your next plans.

Be courageous

You recognize that you are no longer a fit for partnership with this person. It's helpful to acknowledge that you and this other person put a certain amount of energy and time into the relationship. Even so, now it's time to make a change.

It takes courage to design a partnership that supports you. Your aim is to continue to be truthful, clear and flexible along the way. Keep checking in with yourself since your needs may change from moment to moment. Know that whichever process you choose, you get to design it. Aim to move forward with respect for each other and recognition for what each of you has been through.

Recognize the end

Make sure that your partner is clear that the relationship (as it was) is ending. Realize that you are moving from one life chapter to another. When you are in completion mode, whatever that may look like to you, make sure you and the other person know that the breakup is happening. If, after a conversation, one person begins mourning and the other sees that conversation differently, you may have to discuss the breakup again. This out-of-sync timing can feel challenging and disheartening. Make sure you both recognize the change together. Name it, acknowledge it, and then see what comes next. The end may be a conversation or it may be a ritual lighting of a candle or a silent walk in the woods. If what you did together didn't feel conclusive enough for you, remember you can design more steps to support you individually or with friends or family.

Let go of resentments, apologize, forgive: Is there something lingering that you could let go of in order for you or your partner to move on more easily? This might be something you resent them for or you wish to apologize for. Maybe there is something you want to forgive them or yourself for.

Once you identify what it is, ask yourself what the best way to release it might be. Consider the impact of sharing each of the following steps directly with your separating partner. Would it be better to talk with a friend who is not your separating partner? Instead you could create a process that would involve talking with a friend or writing a note that you then burn or bury.

> *The disadvantages of sharing resentments with the separating partner are many, and I don't recommend it. I did this once and felt sore from revisiting the hard moments and angry and annoyed about learning new things he had been resenting about me along the way.*

> *I went through all these suggested steps with a friend rather than directly with my partner. My friend listened to the resentments, apologies, what I forgave my previous partner for, what I was grateful for, what I appreciated and what I was learning. Then my friend reflected back what they heard. They acknowledged my honesty, vulnerability and desire to move on beyond this relationship. Letting my partner go in this way felt helpful and I could apologize and forgive more fully.*

Express gratitude, appreciation, and learning

It can be very sweet and beneficial to express gratitude while in each other's presence. You might share a memory you are taking with you or name a quality that your partner brought to the relationship. It can be meaningful to recognize that you both devoted time and energy to this relationship and to end by appreciating these aspects of the experience.

Some possible questions to choose from:
- What are you grateful for?
- What do you appreciate about the other person?
- What is something you'll miss?
- What did you learn from the relationship or the partner?

- What will you take with you to your next romantic relationships?

Make requests with clear timelines

Is there something clear you would like to ask of the other person to support you in moving forward? This might be a kind of connection request, a practical request or it might be for a time without contact.

Here are some examples:

A connection request: You would like to continue a certain aspect of your relationship such as supporting each other's website or dancing Tango together on Tuesdays. You could decide to check in about how it's going in a month.

A practical request: You and your previous partner have a shared bank account. You decide on a deadline by which time each of you will have established a separate account.

A space request: You may frequent the same spaces, attend the same events or share friends. You may not want to see your previous partner for a period of time. Look for ways both parties can still participate in their previously shared community. Maybe you could alternate going to an event and renegotiate this arrangement in two months.

Create a closing ritual: The sky is the limit here for creating something meaningful. Find a way that fits you. You can do this alone. You may ask one friend to sit in for your partner. You may design an event that includes many people you care about. You may pick and choose from the above suggested steps. As you create your own ritual, imagine a clear beginning, middle, and end.

Here are a few examples of activities you might use or combine to make a ritual that supports you:

- **Alone:** Journal, dance, bury something, write a poem, paint, have a silent meditation retreat.

- **With your partner:** Co-create a ceremony in which you light a candle. You could present a song, a painting, or a dance to each other. It may be a verbal process in which you apologize, forgive, or express gratitude. You may share what you will miss about the other. You may thank them for what you have learned or express admiration for what you saw the other one learning. You may share how you request support from each other in moving forward. You may find a moment that symbolizes saying goodbye. This could be shutting off the light, leaving the space separately or ringing a gong.

- **With your community:** You may do any of the previous ceremonial steps in front of a loving group of friends. You may have them say what they appreciated about your partnership and what they'll miss. The community may cut a string that ties you together. They could bless you two as individuals in your next steps. This could be celebrated by holding a joyous dance party.

Let go of shared dreams

It is likely that you have created some plans or dreams with your partner. Now it is time to let go of these in relation to your partner. You may have wanted to take a vacation or planned to create a home together. These dreams never existed in reality. You may have talked about them and so the planning and daydreaming existed, but the dreams themselves were never actualized.

While these fantasies may have been a shared creation, you individually played a key role in forming them. You can take what you want of these dreams with you. Later on you can craft new versions about your future alone, with your community, or with future partners. Knowing what's yours can be empowering.

Look forward

Once you recognize that partnership is no longer what you want with this person, taking the steps to uncouple is an act that is both truthful, compassionate, and generous. Separation often supports both people to move toward the next level of learning and connections. (This may be gaining skills and support to become the partner they wish to be.) While reflection is helpful for a time, it is also imperative to look forward in your own new direction.

Change relationship with your previous partner

Sometimes people are able to shift from being loves/lovers into having new roles with each other. For example, two people in a romantic partnership could become only colleagues, purely dance partners, or just friends. At other times people may need some time apart with minimal communication or even with no contact. The goal is to consciously choose the path that best supports your mourning process and enables you to move forward. Ideally when you next meet your previous partner you can be present to new possibilities of relating to each other.

I have been a part of ending numerous relationships. Many times I had a strong desire to be able to easefully switch to being friends or colleagues instantly after breaking up. This intention was so strong that I often ended up faking that I felt fine. In reality, it didn't actually feel that way at all.

I wanted to be a resilient, loving person and thought that the only way to do that was to stay in close contact directly after the uncoupling. Now I recognize that I prefer to be truthful. That means I make different choices at different times. Directly after a breakup, I often consider taking time apart before re-engaging. I recognize that by taking space first, I can more honestly consider being my previous partner's friend later on.

Find support

For some time after the chapter of being a couple ends, it is normal to notice memories and emotions arising, sometimes unexpectedly. It's important to recognize this is part of the journey forward.

You might need to seek support to heal. Here are some possibilities:
- support circles
- a therapist
- a friend who knows how to listen

You might seek support to move forward:
- a friend to talk about possibilities with
- a friend to do activities with
- self dates
- vision quests
- a self help book or workshop
- a new hobby
- a life coach

Examples of recognizing a need and finding support

- You watch a movie that reminds you of a special moment with your previous partner. You feel intense emotions so you call a friend to listen to you for a while. You talk about the movie and your experience. Your friend reflects what they heard and affirms that you are doing well in this mourning process.

- You have decided to go out with some mutual friends and your previous partner will be there. On the day before the plan you feel uneasy. You listen to your body cues and reevaluate what would best nourish you. You want to show up well to the people in your community. You consider instead calling up another friend to spend the evening with.

Pick a self-date activity that can nourish you

- Go on a solo hike
- Take a yoga class or workshop
- Take yourself out for dessert
- Give yourself body time: Get a massage, a bubble bath, solo sexy time
- Go up high and watch the sunrise/sunset
- Make art (painting, pottery...)
- Go to a favorite spot and do something special there (journaling at a tea shop)
- Browse a thrift shop

Re-establish relationships with others

Remember that your friends and family (biological or chosen) are still around and probably want to connect with you. Let them know that you care about them. They may also have feelings and thoughts about your relationship or your breakup. Clearly letting them know what you are available for in supporting them and what support you are asking for from them can enable your connection to deepen at this vulnerable moment.

Spend time together

Some friends may be used to seeing you only with your previous partner, seemingly acting as one unit together. They may feel that they don't know you as a separate individual. If this is the case, you having time alone with them may be helpful in reestablishing your relationship. Create new memories together.

Tell your friends and family how to support you

Your friends, with all their good intentions, may offer something that is unhelpful.

> *KJ says to Hannah "I saw the breakup coming. He wasn't good to you. He was always criticizing you. I'm glad you ended that one."*

Hannah: I was annoyed that my friend said this to me. Now, I felt like I needed to help her to understand me rather than being able to receive her support. I wanted to defend my previous partner and felt unprepared to do so. I could still see him as awesome at times and did not want to collude with my friend's story or opinion.

Set your friends up to support you by clarifying how, before you meet. It might sound something like this.

"Thanks for supporting me. I am still in the process of getting over this relationship. Right now, I don't want to hear your opinion about the breakup or my previous partner. You can support me simply by listening to me as I share my sadness that the relationship is not what I had hoped for. I'd love hugs, to cook a meal together, and to hear about your life. Are you open to that?"

Tell them what you can and cannot offer them

Your friends or family may also need some support to let go of the image or dreams they had of your partnership. However, it should not be up to you to provide that support. Tell them that you wish for them to find support elsewhere and maybe make a few, caring suggestions.

My grandfather had a phone call with my ex-fiancé to offer support to him after we broke off the arrangement. I'm still unclear who was supporting whom in that chat and only heard that it had happened years later. I'm so happy they could do what they needed without my involvement.

Reclaim personal connection to places, activities, and objects

In addition to people, memories often get linked to places, activities and objects.

A few examples:
- You enjoy hanging out with two friends who are a couple. Ever since you began dating your previous partner, you would only see this couple on a double date. Now it seems awkward to be with them alone.

- The only times you have eaten at one particular Thai restaurant you have been with your previous partner, so it feels connected to being together.

- You never snacked on seaweed crackers before this relationship. Now whenever you see a package of seaweed crackers you can't help but remember being cuddled up on the couch, crunching, while watching late night movies.

- Your previous partner gave you the house slippers you used to wear constantly. That pair has now been retired to the closet. It's getting cold and you may want to wear slippers soon.

- You drive by the mountain you hiked last year every Sunday and remember the incredible view you shared with your previous partner.

It's normal that these memories are linked to your previous partner, at least up until now. However, when you are ready, you can gently begin to create new memories with these objects, activities, and places. They can be both connected to meaningful memories with your former partner and also be a part of your independent life moving forward.

What would you like to leave behind and what would you like to have as part of your life still? Do you begin to wear the slippers again or do you choose a different style and buy yourself a new pair? Maybe you take a friend up that same mountain or take yourself out to Thai food on a solo date. Perhaps you hang out with your friends separately or in a larger group so you don't have the worry of being 'a third wheel'. You might even introduce a new date to late night movie snacks of seaweed and find out if they enjoy them as much as you do.

Soon after one important relationship ended, I traveled through several cities and communities that my previous partner and I had explored together. I decided to confront the feelings that came up and found that I appreciated this opportunity for mourning. As an independent person I was making fresh connections to the places and people I had seen before. I could feel the past at the same time as I was making new memories.

Three months later, I was surprised when my former partner sent me some sweet texts of memories he had of being in these special places together. It turned out, he had been in one location working intensively during the months directly after our breakup. He was just beginning his process down memory lane, both mourning and celebrating. We were out of sync in our individual processes, but both of us, in our own time, found value in reclaiming our personal connections.

You have read through ways to celebrate and heal during the uncoupling process alone, with community or with your previous partner. Most people go through both of these stages and may do so in a non-linear way. You have explored some of the many ways to find support to move forward with your next life steps. Given all this, how would you design a successful way forward for you?

Uncoupling: Key points

Fundamentals

> Make sure you stay safe through the breakup
> Tune into your own needs and choose how to go forward
> Make sure both parties recognize the ending

Suggested process steps (alone, with partner, with others)

> Let go of resentments, apologize, forgive
> Express gratitude, appreciation, and learning
> Let go of shared dreams
> Make requests with clear timelines
> Create a closing ritual

Create a new relationship with your previous partner

> Assess whether or not you need time apart
> Consider whether you shift to colleagues or friends

Find support for healing and moving forward

> Make self-dates
> Re-establish relationships with others
> Teach others how to support you
> Reclaim personal connection to places and events

Polyamory

You may feel more individual agency and experience more satisfaction by recognizing that you have many options within 'polyamory.' You may be asexual, sexual or hypersexual or any unique version of you along the spectrum of categories. Regardless of where you are on your journey with love and sex, this chapter is written for you in hopes that you gain insights as you courageously and creatively design relationships that show care for everyone involved.

All healthy relationships take ongoing attention and skill regardless of the structure. Living a life of polyamory adds extra layers of complexity to the existing joys and challenges of managing one romantic relationship. In polyamorous relationships there are more people you may be impacting that you want to consider.

In some cases polyamory has come to be linked with a reputation of people who have lots of sex without having the awareness or skills to care for the people involved. In addition to this unethical promiscuity reputation, many anecdotes tell stories of poly novices who bravely attempted to be intimate with more than one person without the support or skills necessary for success. While these heartbreaking stories have validity, people have different approaches to polyamory and everyone starts as a beginner. It is important now to share more resources and tools so that we can make informed choices that more consistently support everyone involved.

Many kinds of relationships can be described as ethical including polyamorous ones. In this chapter you will find an explanation of polyamory, a recognition of the societal messages of romantic relationships that most of us have been exposed to, and tips to try during your dynamic relationship trajectory. You can find suggestions and examples of how support networks may look and how you may talk about polyamory at the level of openness or privacy that suits you.

It takes a lot of courage to challenge the status quo. It takes effort and motivation to really look at the personal things that arise. The choice to explore polyamory is likely to support you to be a resilient, aware person and to become the partner you want your partners to have.

Polyamory: What is it really?

Polyamory includes any relationship exploring love and/or sex with more than one person that consciously uses consent and agreements between everyone involved. There are many ways this can look and feel. Since polyamorous relationships may or may not include sex or romance, relationships can be made up of people with a wide range of romantic or sexual expression and desires. People may identify as hypersexual, sexual, or asexual. They may also use "hyper-romantic," romantic, or "aromantic" to describe themselves.

People may identify as 'polyamorous' or 'non-monogamous' or a number of other similar labels regardless of their current relationship structures. At the moment they may be single or partnered to one or many people. There are infinite ways to live these relationships and no right number of partners to have.

What does *ethical* mean in this context? This is a hugely debated topic in polyamorous cultures today. Given that we all make mistakes and hurt others, we need our own ethical compass to evaluate our actions, and each person's compass or definition may differ from the next.

To me, being ethical means:
- I am willing to look at the effects my actions have on others.
- If I become aware that harm is being done or if my partners are not satisfied with what is happening, I am willing to seek to change the situation.
- When I make decisions, I consider everyone involved.
- I am willing to have truthful conversations about how I am living out polyamory.

Societal messages:

Mainstream US society marginalizes polyamorous relationships along with many other kinds of relationships that break social conventions. It is an exciting time when brave people are challenging the mainstream norms and publicly loving in ways that are right for them. We can observe this social change today especially in comparison to the messages the majority of us grew up with. Most people were surrounded by examples of monogamous relationships that demonstrated what has come to be referred to as the 'relationship escalator.' This is the idea that once you enter a relationship you have few options and will most likely keep ascending in order, following this step-by-step linear process:

Relationship escalator steps:
1. Begin to date
2. Become exclusive, sexually and romantically
3. Get married (if legally sanctioned where you live)
4. Create a home to live in together
5. Have kids (possibly)
6. Remain together until death or divorce

Most people are taught to believe this sequence is the way intimate relationships are supposed to work and that emotionally balanced adults 'should' want to take those steps. While this may be exactly the life that some people want and enjoy, love is not a one-size-fits-all experience.

Research shows that 40-50 percent of US marriages end in divorce and that infidelity is common. While 'infidelity' can be defined in many ways, Esther Perel (psychotherapist and author) says that for the wounded spouse, it is an experience of betrayal. This data not only demonstrates how common it is for relationships to become unethical, but also inspires further questioning of what would adequately prepare and support people to maintain truthful relationships. Some believe that if people become aware of their options, if the stigma attached to polyamory decreases and if people learn key communication skills, relationships will thrive in ways that better serve everyone involved and the number of affairs will decrease.

Needs met by having multiple partners (a few examples)

If, while dating a person who is open to polyamory, you discover that only some of your needs are met within the relationship, clarify what you are willing to offer each other. Then discuss together what you might look for in other areas of your lives. Going camping with one person, attending sensual dance retreats with others, and having multiple lovers may all be possible with honesty and coordination. Here are a few examples:

- Different sex drives: One member of a romantic partnership is asexual and the other sexual. Both can get their needs met.

- Different sexual desires/ practices: One person may want to be tied up and spanked and the other feels uncomfortable with scenes like this.

- Different hobbies: One person loves tango dancing and wants to dance with their romantic partner but the other person doesn't enjoy dancing.

- Different spiritual/religious practices: One person wants to share their religious/spiritual practice with their partner and their beliefs differ.

While in relationship/s

In order to develop healthy relationships, it's crucial to develop and apply the many important skills which make multiple connections thrive. The intention is to find the relationships that fits for you, related to the skills and support you have available. A key question to ask yourself is: How much time and attention do I have available right now to offer others?

Care for yourself

To show up well to the other people involved in your intimate interpersonal relationships you must first care for yourself. A few questions you can ask yourself are:

- Have you defined clearly what you want?
- Have you done the healing you might need to move beyond old hurts?
- Do you currently have the support system to turn to when you recognize complex thoughts and charged emotions (such as jealousy) that might be getting in your way of moving forward?

Given your answers to those questions, what community support and resources would help you thrive?

Put people before structures

Relationships work best when all people feel empowered to advocate for their own needs and can design their partnership. Sometimes people get caught up in maintaining a pre-set rule or power dynamic of a certain polyamorous structure rather than putting people first.

One poly structure that is often seen as unethical is called veto power. Veto power is a relationship agreement usually made between primary partners. Veto power gives each member of the primary relationship the power to end a secondary relationship or in some cases set rules about specific activity with the other partner/s.

A primary partnership is a relationship that has more involvement with each other than with their other partners (secondary or tertiary partners). The primary partnership may have more emotional bond or practical commitments with each other and the power of this relationship is considered greater than that of the other relationships the two individuals may have.

Jaquoya and Yin are primary partners who use veto power.

Yin is interested in another person, Julian. Jaquoya tells Yin what he is allowed to do with Julian. Julian has no say in this conversation and Yin does not speak up to negotiate on his own or Julian's behalf because of having committed to veto power.

Julian begins the relationship with Yin but soon starts to feel limited by Joquoya's demands about what they do and don't do together. Eventually Julian ends it because he wants to be in relationships where everyone has an equal say.

The above power dynamic is not only unethical, it is likely to lead to a challenging relationship with unclear communication. In situations like this, all the people involved need to be encouraged to share what they want and to negotiate agreements equally with the other people involved. People should take responsibility for their desires and actions, and be clear that everyone involved is acting consensually.

Act in alignment with what you want and need

It is incredibly helpful to clarify what is truly wanted in partnerships or relationships. Once we know what we are looking for, we can make choices based on those qualities and are more likely to find good fits sooner. This, of course, is not limited to polyamorous people. When there are more people involved, the relationship structure gets put to the test sooner. It is important to put the value of the relationships above the idea of having a set construct of polyamory. If you have one well-suited partner for a time and don't have another lover yet, that may be more successful than having an ideal number of lovers who are not actually good fits.

Getting clear

Alyssa: I have had many different kinds of 'open relationships.' I value having deep intimate connections that include romance, sex, and emotional connection. After ending an important deep primary partnership, I began to date three non-monogamous people. I was investigating distributing my needs amongst these three, hoping to have my desires for partnership covered.

I soon realized that the real question for me was "Am I connecting deeply in the ways I most want?" After thinking this through, I could see that I was not finding the depth of connection I was looking for. I then changed all three relationships. Each one shifted to become only my friend or colleague. I returned to looking for a new romantic partner.

It was clear that, while I might find multiple partners, the most important thing for me is having my desires for connection deeply met. I began looking for one love. Starting there was a relief. Having one aligned romantic partner is more satisfying than having many relationships that don't quite fit. It was important to me that I put the qualities I wished for in a partner before a construct of having many partners or any polyamorous identity label.

Put the needs of everyone involved before strategies

People sometimes have a fixed idea of what is "fair," or stick to one strategy without questioning it. Fairness is a valuable intention to bring to any relationship, yet remaining firm to a concept can at times be more harmful than helpful. Being present to the current needs of the people involved can lead to more flexible thinking.

One example is when couples focus on tallying how many nights or dates each person has with their other lovers. Practically speaking, this method is unlikely to lead to success. Life is unpredictable, and trying to make things entirely the same for each person may not be helpful. For example, one partner may be quite sick and need more support. This causes the tally to be thrown off and instead care, love, and flexibility by all the partners are needed. The aim is not to equal the score. The goal is to do the best possible to see that everyone involved gets support and attention when they need it.

Celebrate your partnerships by tuning your attention to the specific needs of the people involved. "People are not commodities; ethical relationships recognize the humanity, needs and desires of each individual involved" (Veaux, Franklin, & Rickert, 2014).

Suggestions for living in polyamorous relationships

- When you become aware of concerns, ask to discuss them right away.

- Make sure everyone is aware of the elements of the relationship. This transparency is essential for informed consent in healthy relationships.

- Make sure you are not adding a new relationship because the current one has challenges to work on. An old one is not remedied by adding a new one.

- Pay attention to everyone involved. When something comes up that involves someone else, talk directly to that person rather than through another person. This helps avoid incorrect assumptions and avoids having one person be the intermediary. It can also be useful to have a group conversation so you all hear the content firsthand.

- When you are curious about adding a new person into your relationship, find out about the new person's communication skills and how well they are managing their pre-existing relationships.

- Remain flexible. Relationships are dynamic and can frequently change. Life is unpredictable. A few examples: your mother-in-law needs support, a niece is born, or one of you begins mourning a breakup with another partner. If you agree to explore together and acknowledge the shifts rather than ignore life's changes and challenges, a healthy lasting relationship is more likely to develop.

Create a sustainable poly network of support

By taking a look at our closest relationships we can celebrate both what we offer each other and also the variety of ways we create a network of support. Instead of turning night after night to the same person for emotional support, for example, we can enjoy calling up our closest platonic partner one night and cuddling up with our local romantic partner on the next. By spreading requests for support among different people we can experience more ease and feel more available to support others.

Here are some of the many ways we might seek intimacy and connection with different people. It's possible to choose from the selection and mix and match to form all sorts of sweet relationships. These relationships will contribute to your life and enable you to contribute to theirs. For more ideas look up the 'Relationship Anarchy Smorgasbord'.

- Romantic
- Domestic
- Sexual
- Kink (may include sexual energy or not)
- Tantra
- Touch intimacy
  cuddles, dance, massage
- Emotional intimacy and support
- Being seen as a couple in public
- Collaborative/creative partners
- Business partners
- Sharing finances
- Co-caregivers or co-parents
- Friendship
- Life partner

Choose your level of being public or private

It is possible that someone you know is polyamorous but not public about it. There are many reasons why people need to remain private about being non-monogamous. Some people may risk their jobs, child custody or even their lives. The lack of positive modeling mixed with stories of hardship, myths, and minimal information available can lead to fear and confusion on the topic.

Fortunately, more people who can safely come out as polyamorous or non-monogamous are doing so. This may have a larger impact on society than we know. It comes down to human relationships. Some link the big shift in passing laws to support gay rights to the fact that many more voters knew someone who was gay.

Coming out as poly to the family: Alyssa's story

I told my parents and my sister that I was exploring a number of romantic and sexual relationships. This brought up worries for my dad. I imagined that underneath his fear he was caring for me and my well-being. I imagined that he was concerned about me choosing a hard life, taking many health risks and that I would not find the future I envisioned. My dream has always included having a stable loving lifestyle that supports me individually. It also includes having children and collaborating on parenting. In this moment, it became clear that my dad's vision for me had been that I could and would do this with only one man.

I suggested we go around and share a little personal update. The conversation went something like this:

> *Alyssa: I want to share with you that I am dating three interesting people right now. One lives locally and the other two are long distance. I told you I'm going on a trip soon. That's to visit one of them.*

> *Dad: That sounds like that thing called polyamory! (Emphasizes 'polyamory' as though other worldly).*

> *Alyssa (calmly): Yeah, that's exactly what it is. I am polyamorous.*

Dad: Woah. That sounds so hard. I remember mom and I considered living with another family and it ended up that they had a messy divorce. I was glad we didn't raise kids together.

Sister (ally): Dad, I know you really care about 'Lyss. We were hearing her update and she shared something really important to her. This moment reminds me of the frequent experience people have when they come out as gay and their people respond by telling their own stories instead of acknowledging the person who vulnerably just came out. Maybe you are just wanting the best for 'Lyss and worried about her?

(Dad breathes deeply.)

Sister continues: Did you finish what you were saying, 'Lyss?

Alyssa: Thanks. Dad, I get that you might be nervous or worried about me but actually I wanted you all to hear how well my life is going. I am happy and healthy and excited to be trying out new lifestyle possibilities. I also feel really honored to support many people in my coaching work who are navigating non-monogamous relationships and feel great about contributing in this way.

While my dad and I have different ideas of how I might best go about my life, after this conversation he was able to see that I am consciously choosing a way of life that works for me. Acknowledging that my dad's intentions are caring intentions was step one. He fundamentally wishes me to be loved and safe. These realizations supported our ability to stay connected when discomfort came up in this conversation.

Coming out to your families

I share this story because families and loved ones may be very new to concepts of non-monogamy. If they are willing to learn from us, we may help them learn about our lifestyles while having compassion for them if they worry or have concerns. By demonstrating that we value our relationships with them, we can move into knowing each other better in a more easeful way. Remember your current relationships. We don't have to be their teachers and may not want to be.

I suggest keeping these things in mind:

- Ask an ally for support: You may need a friend to support you in preparing, sitting by your side during the conversation, or being with you afterwards.

- Be compassionate: This may be very challenging for your family members to imagine. They may experience some unexpected emotions (shock, sadness, fear, anger).

- Leave some time to be together in the initial conversation. They may need time to take in what you are sharing and ask questions or have their responses be heard.

- Keep your relationships in mind. The people you shared with may need some time before approaching the topic with you again. They might need to mourn who they thought you were becoming. (You might remember it took you quite a while before you decided to share this with them.)

- Notice when family members demonstrate (even in the smallest way) that they are willing to hear about your choices. They may disagree with you or not understand some aspects, and it may take some courage on their part to explore learning more. The first thing to do is to recognize their loving intent.

- Refer them to resources: Encourage them to get support and information from other sources. This may help you continue your current relationships without the added stress of acting as their teacher.

Exploring polyamory is an opportunity to build your communication skills and work on designing the relationships you may dream about. You will be able to set up your relationships generously and nourish them so that they continue to support you and all those you love. This path is not for everyone. It takes a lot of courage to challenge the status quo. Those who choose to create many relationships and foster their ongoing growth with the level of care described in this chapter will surely continue to gain skills for life-long loving and develop more resiliency and ability to share their love widely.

Polyamory: Key points

Challenge society's messages about polyamory

It is not: promiscuity, secret affairs, doomed to failure

Define polyamory clearly and ethically as

Romantic love and/or sex with more than one person
Based on conscious consent of everyone involved
Open and honest
Flexible and endlessly varied to meet people's needs

Use your full communication abilities

As soon as you learn of concerns, discuss them right away
Check that everyone is aware of all of what is going on
Don't try to 'solve' relationship challenges by:
    adding a new lover or
    using pre-set rules or structures (e.g., veto power)
Check a new person's relationship skills and history
    before inviting them in

Care for your relationship/s

Act in alignment with what you want and need
Put the needs of those involved before pre-set strategies
Create a sustainable network of support

Choose whether or how you come out as polyamorous

Choose your right levels of being public or private
Be intentional about how you come out to your family
Be patient with friends and family and with their reactions

Finding your partner

In this chapter you will find suggestions on how to meet someone, some initial questions you might explore, and how to deepen and develop relationships that are good fits. You'll find ways to create the foundation for a truthful, compassionate and integrity-based partnership within a network of supportive relationships you design uniquely for you. This chapter offers options for people who are looking for a variety of relationship structures ranging from polyamorous to monogamous. You may want to read it all or just focus in on the sections that most support what you are looking for.

Get out there and be with other people.

It's important to remember that if you wish to meet other people, it's helpful to be where they gather. Go to a coffee shop instead of working from home. Participate in hobbies that include other people (play volleyball, take a ceramics class, join a book club, go to dance events....).

If you want to meet people with shared interests, go enjoy the thing that lights you up. Maybe they'll spot you there having a blast. If you don't see them, at least you are enjoying yourself.

Tell your community what you are looking for

It gives your friends, colleagues, or family members a chance to play matchmaker successfully.

Choose and use dating applications wisely

There are a variety of dating apps which are cleverly designed to keep your attention. It's easy to get lost looking at images or writing messages and waste a lot of time.

> *Leo: Once, while exploring a dating app, I stayed up all night looking at images and text-message-flirting with random men who ended up just being interested in a sexual thrill and not a deeper*

connection. I was tired and disappointed in myself the following day. I resolved to focus and use my time better.

Know who is doing the filtering

Know the apps' limitations. Each application may require a different approach so that you can efficiently find real prospects.

Mariah: I used the one dating website that includes filters that narrowed my prospects to males who lived nearby within a certain age bracket and were interested in having children. There were other filters to choose from such as institutional education level, smoker, languages spoken, etc.. These filters substantially cut down the number of people I then considered writing to.

On a different dating application with few filters available, there were so many men I could contact that I created my own protocol to reduce the endless introductory chats and save time. I wrote one short note that I pasted in as a message for each prospect early on so as to reveal what I was looking for in partnership clearly. In this way I took on the job of filtering out anyone who was looking only for a hookup. Using this method, I could focus my attention on those who were interested in developing a long-term partnership that would lead to having children together.

Share important elements of who you are from the start

Mariah continued: We met online on Tinder. We were flirtatiously preparing for our first date. I hadn't followed my protocol of asking questions related to my partnership vision. I wanted to clarify what we were each looking for prior to meeting. My text read something like this:

I'm really excited to meet you. I want to share what I am looking for so that we can see what we might be exploring together. I am looking for a deep long-lasting loving and sexual relationship in which we nourish each other to grow together and as individuals. I am looking to have a relationship which can change over time and in alternative ways as we see fit. For instance, we might be open and polyamorous. I also am clear that I want to have children and co-parent together after spending some time developing the relationship. What is your partnership vision?

By having more details about what we were currently interested in before we met, I felt more present and open during the first date. Ultimately, I set myself up for sharing who I am, rather than spending time dating when we might want to be in different scenarios and not realize it.

Acknowledge power dynamics

There may be elements about the roles you each played in the context you first met or the societal privilege differences between you. By naming them together, you can more consciously move forward in a way that actively addresses those elements so that you can treat each other with compassion and respect.

Anastasia: I was excited to connect with Luca, a man I met at a festival I organize. As we began to look at connecting we had a talk about our power differences. We were of the same race and class. We sat down and talked it through.

Anastasia: I want to acknowledge some power differences between us. I recognize I'm an organizer and dance teacher at this festival and you are a helper and participant. I'm eight years older than you.

Luca: I can name that I have privileges as a person appearing CIS gendered and heterosexual male. (CIS gender means that their personal identity and gender corresponds with their birth sex). I also have trained more in Tantra and studied sexuality more than you and so that skillset imbalance may play a role sexually.

After sharing all this we saw that we were capable of connecting as two unique and powerful people who speak their minds and hearts. We committed to keep those factors in mind and agreed to discuss them again if we saw them playing out in our dynamics.

As our relationship continued we recognized more privileges that played a part in different contexts. At some moments having more traditional education played a role. While travelling, one of us had more social network connections and support than the other or more skillsets in a needed area. We aimed to appreciate each other and learn from each other while also recognizing when systemic oppression influenced our relationship and those around us.

Check if you are a fit to explore partnership

When one person is polyamorous and one is monogamous

Silke: A few times over the six years of our relationship, Andy and I had discussed the possibility of opening our relationship to be sexually intimate with others. Each time I brought it up, he was not interested in it and said he felt threatened. I was ok with my choice to continue our monogamous lifestyle. Yet, when marriage was being considered, I realized I was not willing to commit to monogamy until death or divorce do us part. I knew this needed to be said directly and told him so.

Not a fit: In the above pre-marriage story, it was clear that Andy was not open to polyamory during the relationship. This was one way that Silke and Andy were not a match for a relationship. He was looking for a relationship in which both people were monogamous and she was curious to explore intimacy with others.

Find out early on in dating whether you are a fit. Clarify whether both people are interested to some degree in polyamory. After this information is clear, each person can choose to invest their time and energy in relationships with long term potential.

Still interested in partnership: Look to understand the other more and not to change them. Focus on what is possible and seek to gain support and tools for when challenges may arise.

What matters most is that each person is willing to communicate and support each other in having their needs met even when their desires differ. If it is clear that one person wants to be sexually or romantically exclusive themselves and the other wants intimacy with others and they both accept these differences, then proceeding with a partnership may make sense.

Focus on connecting instead of on labels

One approach to support conversation around diverse intimacy desires and practices is to move away from the labels of poly or mono and instead discuss how you each choose to connect to people in your lives.

> *Sue: I'm poly and told Jonah that from the beginning. Jonah was exclusively interested in being romantic and sexual with only me. We imagined we'd have some communication growth opportunities ahead. We were so excited about each other and our vision for partnership that we figured we could sort it out together.*
>
> *We found it helpful to talk about the many ways we seek and get support, nourishment, and intimacy from our friends and community. While he called himself 'monogamous' he acknowledged that he exchanged massages with friends, went out socializing about work over drinks with others, called a specific dear friend for emotional support, practiced his spiritual practice with another community, and came home to me for romance and sex. From this conversation, it was clear that neither of us was exclusive with connection and he seemed to understand me more.*

Get to know each other early on

Share what is important about yourself that may impact the other person's decision to engage more with you. Being clear in the beginning can save a lot of time and confusion.

> *Alyssa: I began a relationship with a man who considered himself monogamous. In an early conversation I shared a few key points about me that might have a direct impact on him.*
> - *I am polyamorous.*
> - *I am known in the community as a support for poly people.*
> - *When you meet my community, people may assume you are also poly.*
> - *I don't have a set construct or vision of how being poly plays out for me. I anticipate my choices shifting throughout our relationship. I intend to discuss my interests with you as they change.*

Ask key questions

In this section you will find flow charts of dialogues filled with questions. This choose-your-own-adventure format is a guide to questions you can ask as you get to know someone you are interested in. There is no one order or way to have these conversations. You may imagine yourself on a date with someone you know or don't know yet and create a one act play in which you are the star.

What's your intention for connecting?

If you are looking for a spiritually-connected long-lasting partnership and they want a sexy kinky fling it's good to find that out early on. Then, being much more informed, you can ask - is there still something to explore here? Maybe you become friends or artistic collaborators or maybe you thank them for the coffee and wish each other well. Being able to state your own needs for connection and at the same time being willing to listen to the other person's needs is a great way to support each other in developing potential long-lasting relationships.

Initial questions

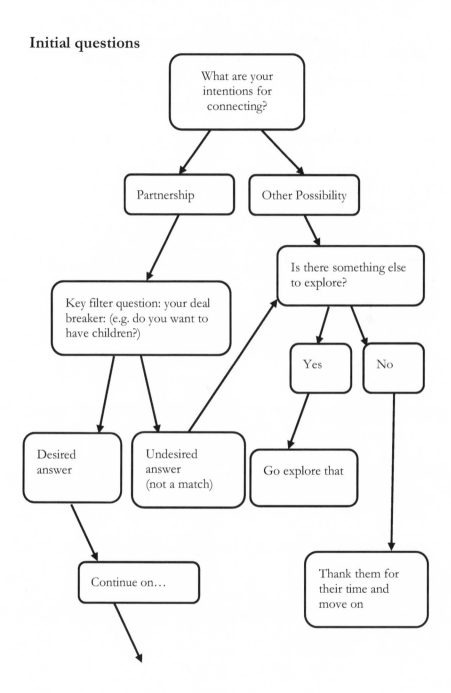

How do you identify sexually and/or romantically?

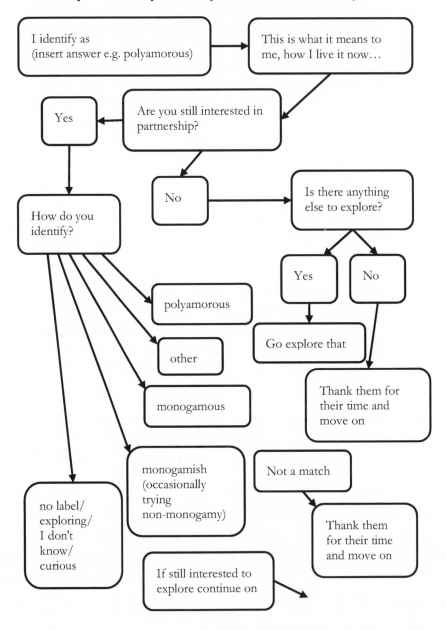

Start by sharing your identity, how you are living currently or what you are looking for in terms of love, sex, and partnership with one or more people. Knowing this early is a helpful piece of information as you discuss whether partnership is in store for you.

It is possible here that you are not a fit based on the kind of relationship you are each looking for. On the other hand, you may have different or similar identities and still decide you are interested in exploring further. If you are in some way exploring polyamory here are some questions that may support your next conversations.

Polyamory questions

- What is your experience with polyamory or non-monogamy?

- What excites you about being open to intimacy with others while being in a relationship with me?

- What worries come up for you about being open to intimacy with others while being in a relationship with me?

What is your thinking about veto power?

This is often a deal-breaker for polyamorists and it's good to know upfront about people's beliefs on this approach to hierarchy in relationships. Some believe it is unethical to use veto power and therefore avoid it.

Veto power is a relationship agreement usually made between primary partners.

A primary partnership is a relationship that has more entwinement with each other than with their other partners (secondary or tertiary partners). The primary partnership may have more emotional bond or practical commitments with each other and the power of this relationship is considered greater than that of the other relationships the two individuals may have.

Veto power gives each member of the primary relationship the power to end a secondary relationship or in some cases set rules about specific activity with the other partner/s.

A story of veto power:

Chen: Shamayla and I had been partners for a while and decided to have veto power because we thought this would support our relationship to never break.

Shamayla: When Chen began falling for Pamela, I met Pamela and approved of them having a relationship. Veto power means that regardless of whether I had said yes or no, Chen would have followed my choice and communicated it to Pamela. Pamela had way less say in the decision.

Chen: 3 years later, Shamayla had a falling out with Pamela and told me I needed to end my partnership with Pamela. I was heartbroken but broke it off because Shamayla and I had committed to have veto power and I didn't want to lose Shamayla. This either/or scenario disregarded the years of relationship I had with Pamela and the depth of love we experienced. It was the hardest thing I've ever done and I felt more distanced from Shamayla afterwards.

How open are you in public spaces about being in multiple relationships?

Each person has the right to decide about their situational openness and may have different considerations about the impact of being seen with multiple partners.

Simona: One person I dated said, if it were purely up to him, he would be open in his town and even affectionate with me in sight of his high school students. His primary partner was working in the local government. She asked him to limit his affection with other lovers in public because she feared for her job.

Is there anything you'd like me not to share or show with others?

This also is a personal choice and there might be some possible consequences we are not aware of. It's good to ask ahead just in case and have a conversation about it if applicable.

Are you dating or in partnership with anyone else currently?

Another partner of my lover is called my 'metamor.' I am also their metamor. This term acknowledges that we share one intimate in common regardless of whether we have ever spoken or met. Some people choose to know a lot about the people their partner is intimate with; others choose to know little. The way a metamor lives and acts will likely impact your life and vice versa. Therefore, starting by asking some key questions about your potential metamors could be helpful. What would be good for you to know about them?

Do we overlap in community? Or might we overlap?

This question is important as it considers the impact on others. Are there previous relationships to consider such as employer/employee, past lovers, or therapist/client? Many of these professions have an ethical code of conduct for the employers themselves but how partners engage may be an area that needs extra consideration.

Also acknowledge the current power dynamics and consider what may be appropriate given those.

If we do have a prior relationship with a potential metamor or other important person in this potential lover's life, would it be wise to check in with the others involved before deepening this relationship?

Betty: One time I played in a kink scene with a coaching client of my primary partner. I had only considered the person as a potential friend of mine and forgotten that he worked at some point with my partner. It caused my partner frustration and I apologized. Now I think this through more carefully before I connect intimately with others.

Polyamory questions

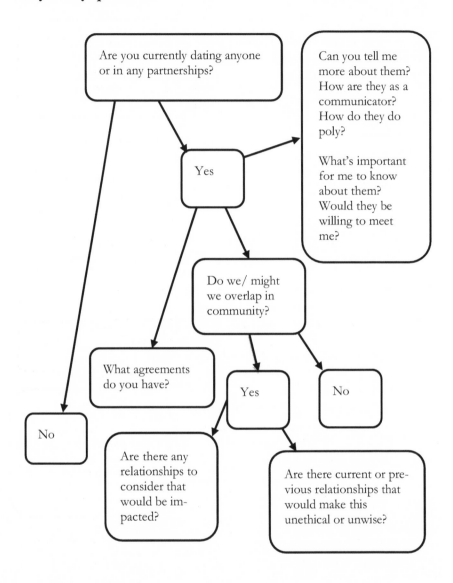

Questions related to sex

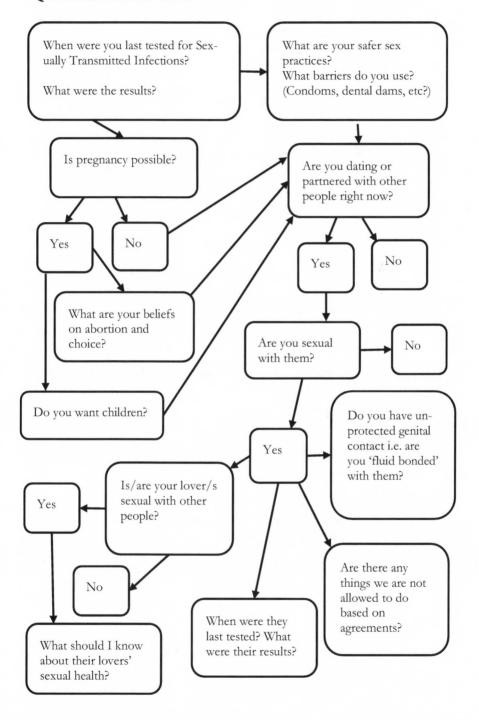

There are many other great questions that might be helpful to ask prior to engaging sexually. You could ask about how they experience gender, what they prefer to call their genitals, what they are interested in exploring and what is completely not their thing. This is just the beginning of creating a satisfying unique and conscious experience. Refer to Zahava Griss's article '8 Steps to Creating the Intimate Explorations You Love' for more great ideas.

Questions about time

These questions are especially helpful for couples that include at least one poly person.

How do you navigate special events in your life with your partners?

Maybe one person spends Christmas Eve with one partner and Christmas day with another. This is designed by each person ideally with all their family members and partners in mind.

What events coming up will you include me in? What events will you exclusively attend with your other partner/s?

It might be helpful to know upfront that Christmas is a celebration that will only include your new partner and their other partner and their shared children. Knowing that you will not be invited to that special event on December 25th you can arrange other ways to celebrate and have clear expectations.

How do you schedule your time with all your loves (and family)?

People who devote themselves to multiple relationships often discuss the limitation of time and the challenge of scheduling. Some people use shared google calendars so that they can both go on dates with others on the same night and still spend time together regularly.

How do you arrange sleepovers with your partners, homes and families?

Chelsea:I dated a man who was in a polyamorous marriage. After I had a lovely dinner with his wife and him, she went up to bed and we took our cuddling from the couch to make out in a nearby park. He told me that while his wife sleeps with her lover in the guest room when he is upstairs in earshot, he prefers to have his lovers over for sleepovers when she is away.

To conclude here, there is no right way to find a partner. This is a creative experience and the more you give it your all, the more you can stay in the game of your life with energy and motivation. Go forth with your enthusiasm, courage, and vulnerability. Date people whose intentions match yours. Ask the important questions that apply to you in time to know clearly if you are moving forward together with clarity and alignment. These questions are only some of the many ways to engage your curiosity with a new person. By being truthful early on, you can be generous to yourself and to the other people involved. You will be able to look back and know you showed up in ways that you are proud of.

Find your partner: key points

Get started

    Tell your community what you are looking for
    Choose and use dating applications wisely
    Share key elements of who you are from the start
    Acknowledge power dynamics

Check if you are a fit to explore partnership

    Explore if your relationship intentions are compatible
    Address sex and romance identity questions (flow chart)
    Address polyamory relationship questions (flow chart)
    Address questions about safe sex (flow chart)

Questions for a new polyamorous relationship

    Decide whether "veto power" serves us
    Discuss when and where to be public vs. private
    Consider how best to divide time among all relationships

Resources for chapter 6

Today, there are more resources becoming available to support people to consider and explore a variety of options in order to learn about communication, relationships, and polyamory. In addition to books, websites and podcasts may be great resources for you. There are polyamorous counselors, coaches, meetups and support groups. They each offer various approaches and a range of support. I'll share some resources that have influenced my thinking and inspired me. I wish you a fun journey into the abundant list of possibilities

And please remember to reach out to me if I can support you or your loved ones in any way.

alyssalynescoaching@gmail.com
https://alyssalynes.com

Communication and personal growth skills

Chapman, Gary. (1992) *The 5 Love Languages: The Secret to Love that Lasts*. Chicago, IL: Northfield Publishing. As a #1 New York Times Bestseller for 8 years running, many readers have used the examples and questions in this book to discover their own love language. Chapman suggests that better communication between couples can be accomplished once both people can demonstrate care to their partner in ways the recipient can understand.

Katie, Byron. (2019) Available from https://thework.com/ A clear website to get an overall understanding of her four-step process to identify and question any thoughts that might be seeming to have power over us. Byron Katie describes "The Work" as an answer to the question of how to move toward freedom.

Levine, Amir and Heller, Rachel. (2010) *Attached: Are you Anxious, Avoidant or Secure? How the Science of Adult Attachment Can Help You Find - and keep - love. New York, NY:* Tarcher. As the first book on Attachment theory as it relates to adult romantic relationships, the book *Attached* guides readers to identify which attachment style they and their partner follow. While this 'science of love' should not be considered in isolation, it is indeed an insightful and supportive approach to find and maintain loving relationships.

Lynes, Alyssa. Show up in Ways You Are Proud of: A Coaching Group to Help You Enjoy Your Romantic Relationships. Retrieved from https://alyssalynes.com/coaching-group This intimate online bi-monthly coaching group for polyamorous people supports folks to find clarity and take action so as to experience more grace, joy and ease in their sexual and romantic relationships.

Martin, Betty. (n.d.). The Wheel of Consent [videos]. Retrieved from https://bettymartin.org/videos/ This is an extensive webpage of resources that includes a free seven-hour video training full of explanations and fun exercises about receiving and giving pleasure and developing an awareness of whom the experience is for. The page provides worksheets and videos to support you to teach the material and where to learn more.

Nemeth, Maria. Mastering Life's Energies Course. (Academy for Coaching Excellence). Retrieved from https:// acecoachtraining.com/ MLE is a four-day course that is offered most frequently in CA, USA and Sweden. The intensive course supports purpose-driven people to identify and master their personal internal stopping points. Participants learn new skills to make the contribution they are here to make and how to empower others to do the same.

Nemeth, Maria. (2007). *Mastering Life's Energies: Simple Steps to a Luminous Life at Work and Play. Novato, CA: Neworld Library.* This life-changing book provides new skills to approach life with a willingness to live it vibrantly and with a sense of contribution. It supports readers with practical methods to see where they truly are and where they want to go.

Patterson, K. and Grenny, Joseph, et ál. (2012). *Crucial conversations: Tools for talking when stakes are high.* New York: McGraw-Hill. This powerful guide provides key tools that have revolutionized how people prepare for and have high-stake conversations in their personal and professional lives. It contains many useful anecdotal examples for multiple contexts.

Rosenberg, Marshall B. (2015). *Nonviolent Communication: A Language of Life: Life-Changing Tools for Healthy Relationships.* Encinitas, CA: PuddleDancer Press. An important guide to a perspective and practice of compassion to increase our ability to live with meaning, connection, and choice. While traveling internationally, I found NVC to be a fundamental strategy for connection in community building projects and as a support to sustain intimate relationships.

The Center for Nonviolent Communication. Available from https://www.cnvc.org/ The website provides information on the technique and where to learn it.

Tobi, Zo. Give Yourself to Love: A Love and Partnership Course for Progressives and Changemakers. Retrieved from https://zo-tobi.com/love/ This pay-what-you-can online course taught by Masterful coach, Zo Tobi, is both spiritual and practical in approach. The course provides both trainings and coaching and has a profound effect on people's ability to find and grow the partnership they would love.

Polyamory

Carrellas, Barbara. "Non-Monogamy, Open Relationship, and Polyamory Resources." *Urban Tantra* Retrieved September 23, 2019, from http://barbaracarrellas.com/wp-content/up-loads/2011/01/Polyamory-Resources.pdf Barbara is a heartfelt facilitator and author of the book *Urban Tantra*. I have learned a great deal from her in areas of self love and connection. This page lists books and online resources on polyamory.

Easton, Dossie and Hardy, Janet W (2017) *The Ethical Slut, (3rd ed.): A Practical Guide to Polyamory, Open Relationships and Other Freedoms in Sex and Love.* SF, CA: Greenery Press. Originally published in 1994 this has acted as a groundbreaking book to dispel myths and offer responsible, safe and fun methods to live a life of polyamory.

Freedman, Mia (Producer) (2017, October 8). No Filter: Esther Perel Knows Why People Cheat [Audio Podcast] Retrieved from https://player.fm/series/series-2342957 In this podcast interview, Esther Perel gives an overall clear explanation of why so many people struggle with infidelity and contextualizes polyamory in her perspective on culture.

Griss, Zahava (2018, June 25), Clarifying Agreements Before you go Play, [Blog Post] Retrieved from https://www.embody-morelove.com/blog/clarifying-agreements-before-you-go-play A rich informative article to inspire courageous conversations between partners prior to entering play spaces or festivals where sexual and/or romantic intimacy will be explored.

Griss, Zahava (2016, July 16), 8 Steps to Creating the Intimate Explorations You Love, [Blog Post] Retrieved from https://www.embodymorelove.com/blog/8-steps-to-creating-the-intimate-explorations-you-love A fundamental tool for everyone to bring our intimate relationships to a new conscious level through these inspiring and provocative 8 steps.

Lindgren, Jase, Matlack, Emily and Winston, Dedeker (producers and hosts). (2017, August 22) Multiamory: Six Questions You Must Ask Your New Partner [Audio podcast] Retrieved from https://www.multiamory.com/podcast/133-6-questions-you-must-ask-your-new-partner?rq=MOVIES. A sincere, playful trio discuss acronym tool and how to use it at the start of poly relationships. It includes questions ranging from metamors to scheduling.

Perel, Esther (Producer) (2018) Where Should We Begin? [Audio Podcast] Retrieved from https://www.estherperel.com/podcast This is a unique audio series in which Esther Perel supports partners in a one-time couple's therapy session on topics ranging from illness to infidelity. This range of themes combined with Perel's sincere and straightforward approach offers something meaningful for every listener.

Ryan, Christopher. & Jethá, Cacilda. (June 2010). *Sex at dawn: The prehistoric origins of modern sexuality.* New York, NY: Harper. A thorough examination of prehistoric human sexual behavior revealing many fallacies and weaknesses of previous agreed upon truths.

Sattin, Neil. Relationship Alive [Audio Podcast] Interviews with various experts cover all sorts of topics relating to sex, love, communication, uncoupling, polyamory, dating, healing and more. There is something for everyone.

Schoenfeldt, Alex (2016, December 21)
The Relationship Smorgasbord [Blog Post] Retrieved from http://openrelationshipuniversity.com/the-relationship-smorgasbord/ A helpful visual to categorize and consider the various roles that multiple intimate partners may play in your life.

Veaux, Franklin. & Rickert, Eve. (September 2014). *More Than Two: A Practical Guide to Ethical Polyamory.* Thorntree Press. This is hands down the primary resource book to find strategies and suggestions and to become more aware of the wide range of experiences and possibilities for polyamorous people. Many poly folks call this their 'bible' or go-to book on polyamory. This is a must read for anyone interested in non-monogamy.

Veaux, Franklin. More Than Two [website] Thorntree Press. Available from https://www.morethantwo.com/ This is a rich online resource guide to any facts, basics, and tips on non-monogamy. It also has an extensive helpful glossary of terms.

Wolf, T. (2016) *Ask Me About Polyamory: The Best of Kimchi Cuddles.* Thorntree Press. A realistic, touching and informative comic that covers polyamorous, queer, and genderqueer real-life situations. It is both entertaining and practical.

Conclusion

I am honored to have had the opportunity to share with you some stories and tips from my experiences. I wish for each of us to courageously and at times playfully engage with these possibilities of loving so as to have skilled and sincere relationships. Let's share our best selves with those around us, regardless of their perspectives, communication skills, or if they are older than us or the up and coming generation.

I imagine a world in which we accept each other's different approaches to partnership/s, love, sex, and intimacy. I see people engaging with ease and clarity as they move through their lives, shifting their relationships as they see fit. We decrease our infidelity rate and instead develop resilient and brave strategies so as to have more honest conversations with our loved ones. We consider our impact on each other and find ways to love each other for all that we are regardless of the relationship structure, the distance, the uncoupling transitions or the exciting beginnings of finding each other.

The opportunity to develop ourselves in these out-of-the-box relationships is not a selfish one. We can inspire others to think critically of the status quo and to increase communication skills while developing our creative and compassionate minds and hearts.

Thank you

Thank you to Christopher and Anne for trusting in my ideas and offering all kinds of empowering support during this collaboration. Thank you to Christopher and my mother who edited with me and the friends who read early versions and provided feedback.

I am so grateful to all the partners and lovers I have had who have shared their strategies and have been with me as I developed mine over the years. You have taught me so much and I am thrilled to be able to share my findings with others through this book.

Made in the USA
Middletown, DE
18 November 2019

78956829R00137